# William, I Read Your Book!
## *(God, did you really say that?)*

By

Bill Farrar

ACW Press
5501 N. 7th Ave. #502
Phoenix, AZ 85013

*William, I Read Your Book*
Copyright © 1999
William Farrar
All rights reserved.

Cover design by Eric Walljasper
Page design by Steven R. Laube

All rights reserved. No part of this book may be reproduced in whole or in part without written permission from the author, except by a reviewer who may quote brief passages in a review; nor may any part of this book be reproduced, stored in a retrieval system, or transmitted in any form or by any means electronic, mechanical, including photocopying, recording, or other, without permission in writing from the author, except as provided by USA copyright law.

Unless otherwise noted, all Scripture quotations are from the *Holy Bible*, King James Version.

Scripture quotations marked NIV are taken from the *Holy Bible*, New International Version, copyright © 1973, 1978, 1984 by International Bible Society. Used by permission of Zondervan Publishing House. All rights reserved.

Scripture quotations marked Living Bible are taken from *The Living Bible*, © 1971 owned by assignment by KNT Charitable trust. all rights reserved.

Publisher's Cataloging-in-Publication
*(Provided by Quality Books, Inc.)*

Farrar, Bill (William), 1921-
  William, I read your book : (God, did you really say that?) / by William Farrar — 1st ed.
  p. cm.
  ISBN 1-892525-01-1

  1. Farrar, Bill (William), 1921-  2. Christian life--Anecdotes.  3. Spiritual biography.  4. Dreams--Religious aspects--Christianity.  5. Visions. I. Title

BV4517.F37 1998          248.2 [B]
                         QBI98-1540

Printed in the United States of America

## To My Grand & Great Grandchildren,
## {And anybody else who wants
## to look over my shoulder}

When Kendra was about four years old, her grandmother was explaining to her and Jennifer that she was her granddaughter and Jennifer was her great granddaughter. Kendra took exception to that statement immediately.

She asked, "But, Grandma, aren't I GREAT too?"

Grandma responded, "I think that you are all GREAT, and your grandfather and I wish the best in life for each of you."

The following stories are all true and factual happenings, as much as my memory permits. As I experienced each of them, I learned a new truth. For this reason, I am recording them for you.

Pretend that you are the central figure in each one and listen to the Holy Spirit speak to you personally. As you learn to know God and His never ceasing concern for us, you will trust Him more and more. After all, we can not really trust or have a relationship with someone we don't know.

I believe that God, by His mighty power at work within us, can do far more than we would ever dare to ask or dream of—infinitely beyond our highest prayers, desires, thoughts, or hopes. Let this thought of His immeasurable love and power continually at work in each of us be an insatiable and exciting challenge in your life.

God has given each of you a special unique gift and ability. Desire it, seek it, and use it. You will be laying up imperishable treasures in the eternal heaven. Lastly, I desire that when you stand before God, you will hear Him say, "Well done, good and faithful servant."

May God bless you richly,
Grandpa William Farrar

Heartfelt gratitude to Peter Enns and Carolyn and Bill Simank for their indispensable assistance

# Table of Contents

Preface: Your Heritage ................................................................. 7
1: The Former and the Latter Rains ...................................... 13
2: Dream:Education ................................................................ 16
3: Dream: Give Me This Mountain ...................................... 18
4: Dream: Christmas Gift ....................................................... 23
5: Vision: Surely Goodness and Mercy ............................... 27
6: Dream: Storm, Oppression ............................................... 30
7: Psychology, Psychiatry: Golf ........................................... 32
8: Am I in Your Will? ............................................................. 34
9: Charismatic: Worried About Her Husband .................. 36
10: Job: Vet Medicine Hospital ............................................. 38
11: Dream: Gift, Proposal, Readiness ................................. 41
12: Dream: Happy Days, The Presence .............................. 43
13: Protection: Wasps ............................................................ 45
14: Heresy: Change churches ............................................... 48
15: Nursing Home: Last Chance .......................................... 50
16: Dream: Rod's Coincidence ............................................. 52
17: Deacon: Humor, Seminar ............................................... 55
18: Job: Wait, Surprise .......................................................... 59
19: Vision: Watercolor .......................................................... 63
20: Vision: Memorial Day Flood ......................................... 66
21: Vic's Dreams: Fasting ..................................................... 68
22: Sonja: Temptation ........................................................... 71
23: Angels: Fleece .................................................................. 74
24: Shaking: Economy ........................................................... 78
25: Jim: Bus Fare, Ride Home .............................................. 80
26: Widow: Sunset, Blessing ................................................ 82
27: Oranges and Potatoes ..................................................... 84
28: Feed My Sheep: 23rd Psalm ........................................... 86
29: Election Time ................................................................... 88
30: Deacon's Son ................................................................... 90
31: Anger: I Quit ................................................................... 92

32: Kathy, Respect: Listening ................................................. 94
33: Kathy: God Hears Prayers .................................................. 96
34: Esoteric ............................................................................... 99
35: Wanda: Overwhelming Fear .......................................... 101
36: Gift of Tongues: Two Reasons ....................................... 103
37: Susie: Another Friend ..................................................... 105
38: Wimber: Seminar on Healing ........................................ 110
39: Paula and Larry: Early Church ...................................... 113
40: Madeleine: Lord Help Me .............................................. 116
41: Pot and Potter: The Voice ............................................... 118
42: Meriam: Divorce, Reconciliation ................................... 120
43: 11, 24, 42: Governments .................................................. 123
44: Aunt Flora: Cancer .......................................................... 125
45: Let Me Know: Jig Saw Puzzle ........................................ 127
46: Stroke: This Is the Day ................................................... 129
47: Crossing the Bar .............................................................. 132
48: Dream: New Beginnings ................................................ 135
49: Shaffer: Enoch ................................................................. 138
50: Sharon: Forgiveness ....................................................... 140
51: My Desire: Schuller ........................................................ 143
52: Heart Attacks: Continuing Stories ................................ 144
53: Oppression: Spiritual Warfare ...................................... 148
54: Open Their Eye: Chariots of Fire .................................. 150
55: Al and Wilbert: God Directs Our Paths ....................... 152
56: Flight: Faithfulness ......................................................... 154
57: Rose: $42 .......................................................................... 156
58: Salt: Witness .................................................................... 158
59: Dream: Naked and Unashamed .................................... 161
60: The Table is Set ............................................................... 164
Epilogue .................................................................................. 167

# Preface

## Your Heritage

Grandpa Daniel Monroe Shumate was born in 1860 in northern Missouri. He moved to an area about three miles north of the Arkansas border close to the very small town of Golden, Missouri, nestled in the Ozark Mountains. There he "sparked" a young woman by the name of Lucy Mae Sparks. In that part of the country, the term "sparked" stood for courted, wooed, or seeked the hand of. He was nine years older than she, which was normal at that time. They were growing in their relationship until he received this letter supposedly written by her:

> at Home
> Golden Mo
> Mr Dan Shumate,
>     I hear that you have been talking about me. and if it is so, I wish you would attend to your own business, and stay away from here I want you to distinctly under Stand that I dont care anything for you, a hint to the wise is sufficent. I hope you will never enter our house again. Please bare this in minde my happiness is dependent on another. and if you do not no what this is I can tell you. it is your walking papers Please dont think hard of me for changing my mind. your former friend
>                           Lucy Sparks

One day they both attended a country social, but he had not been her escort to the affair. She could not understand why he was so aloof and seemed to ignore her. He was deeply hurt and could not understand what had occurred that prompted her to write to him with such animosity. He spoke to a mutual friend about the situation. His friend easily saw thorough the deception and advised Grandpa that your great-great-great-grandmother would never have written such a note.

He talked Grandpa Shumate into speaking to Grandma Shumate directly about the matter. It was then that they realized that someone in the community did not have their best interests in mind.

They were married and homesteaded a forty-acre track of land in the Horse Shoe Bend country along the White River. Their home was a small log cabin built on the top of a hill that provided a panoramic view in every direction. The center core of their first barn was also a log structure.

Every year Grandma faithfully worked in her vegetable garden and potato patch that were about the size of a third of a typical city block. She spent endless hours canning the food required to sustain her family. A fireplace was added to the cabin in 1909, about the same time as the Wright brothers made their first historic flight at Kittyhawk. During her life, she witnessed much of the explosion of knowledge and travel of the twentieth century.

The deed of the earliest acreage they purchased is dated in October of 1883. Through the years, they continued to acquire land in forty-acre tracts. The last purchase they made was in 1919. The farm became a single tract of land of about 300 acres except for about 20 acres of bottom land. This field is now covered by the waters of Table Rock Lake.

Your ancestor D.M. Shumate was far ahead of his time in knowledge concerning the management of livestock and land. He recognized that this was cattle country and the production of crops for market would not be profitable. He rotated his crops, a modern-day practice that was unheard of at that time. He practiced soil conservation with his cultivation methods, mindful of the future consequences of poor production decisions.

Though he had very little formal education, he was recognized to have enough practical intelligence to be elected associate judge of Barry County in 1902. He was a leader in the early development of that part of the country and was an active member in the founding of the rural school in his district. Around the turn of the century, a journeyman carpenter, assisted by my mother who acted as his "go-for," built a two-story addition to the old homestead.

The new addition had three large rooms on the ground floor, a living room, dining room, and bedroom. The upper floor had three large bedrooms. A large porch extended across the front of the structure. It was a novel sight to see such a prosperous homestead at that time in the Ozark Mountains. It was the product of the ingenuity of a man and woman who were true servants to the citizens of Barry County.

Grandma Shumate was very small in stature but large in every thing that was important. I don't remember ever seeing her walk as she went about doing her daily chores. She moved from task to task at a slow trot, all the time singing all her favorite hymns that were a part of her nature. The Shumate family members were strong supporters of the Baptist Church of Golden, Missouri.

Grandma became the mother of Maud in 1891, of William and Florence, twins, born in 1898, and Flora, who arrived in 1901.

Maud became a school teacher at 16 years of age and taught until she married Erskine Chappell shortly afterward. They moved to Montana, where they homesteaded in the wheat country of that developing state.

Grandpa rented a house in Eureka Springs, Arkansas, where William {Bill}, Florence, and Flora attended high school. After his graduation, Bill went to the University of Missouri and graduated from the school of law. In his senior year, he was elected president of the student body. Most of his law practice was before the Appellate Court of the state of New York.

Florence, my mother, moved to Oklahoma, where she became the district manager of a telephone company. It was in this area that she met and married my father, Miles.

Flora moved to Miami, Oklahoma, and attended the business college located in that town. After graduation, she became the bookkeeper for an automobile agency. Clarence Plannett, a young man from Denver, Colorado, became a member of the First Baptist Church where Flora attended weekly services. Two young ladies of that fellowship competed for his attention. Aunt Flora won the man's affection and got the gold metal, a ring that is. Attending their wedding is one of my earliest recollections of any important event in my life.

I was born in Chelsea but soon moved to Claremore, Oklahoma. Dad owned a dry-cleaning establishment. I don't know why we moved from time to time, but we continued to relocate. I began first grade in Miami in 1927. Two years later, the Depression began. We never went without any necessity, but the Depression was a trying time for our family. In the summer of 1930, I spent part of the summer on my grandparents' farm in the Ozark Mountains of southern Missouri.

This was the only time I had a true relationship with Grandpa. As was the yearly custom, family members gathered at the farm for their vacations. We spent each evening seated on the porch, far from the sounds, lights, and commotion of the city. Away from the fast-paced urban environment, we listened to the music of the tree frogs, whipperwills, and insects with their various songs. We watched lightning bugs blink across the yard. We enjoyed an added bonus when the moon cast its silver beams over the scene.

It was very easy to focus on meaningful things in that peaceful environment. Conversation by people with merry hearts often turned from their memories of their early life on the farm to some subject concerning their relationship with the Lord. I loved to listen as they shared their stories. It was stimulating to learn of the events that had shaped their lives and built such godly character in each of them.

Early on the morning of July 9th, I was awakened. Grandpa had passed away suddenly. It was a blessing that the whole family was there on vacation and had a few days together before he left us. I recall some parts of the funeral very clearly, even though I was only nine years old. The casket was on the front porch. The large front yard was filled with folding chairs, all occupied with friends and relatives who had come to mourn our loss. In fact, the crowd was so large there were people standing outside of the fence that bordered the area.

Four large walnut trees that had been planted when the house was constructed and various other species of trees shaded the large crowd. I had no idea that my grandparents had so many friends, but in the later stage of their lives, they had become known as Uncle Dan and Aunt Lucy. They had earned those titles for all of the years they had spent as servants to their community. I recall that a quartet had been engaged to sing Grandpa's favorite number, "The Church in the Wildwood." That song truly pictured the setting.

Shortly after the funeral, Grandma asked Mother if I could stay with her and attend the one-room country school located nearby. I didn't know of her request at that time, and I believe Mother would have agreed quickly except I had a physical problem then that was of grave concern to her. I had been under the care of a physician in Joplin for two or three years. Occasionally, I had spasms during my sleep and my body would become rigid. Whenever it happened, my mother would place me in a tub of water until I relaxed. Mother and Dad finally agreed to let me remain on the farm until I entered high school.

Years later, Mom told me the reason why she had yielded to Grandma's request. She had had a dream that led to her final decision. The Lord came to her in the dream and told her that it would be safe for me to stay with Grandma, that I would NEVER have another spasm. I never did.

I recall many events during the following four years of my life on the farm. Playing checkers in front of the fireplace during the cold winter evenings with John Sparks and hunting with him along the river brings back many happy memories. John was Grandma's nephew and my cousin. He lived with us and was employed to raise the crops and tend the livestock. Although the hard work of cultivating corn, milking cows morning and night, and helping in the hay harvest brings some pleasant remembrances, I never developed a desire to stay on the farm.

Of all my recollections of that period of my life, in retrospect, the single most important one was waking up early in the morning to the sound of my grandmother's voice in conversation with the Lord. It was a daily event just prior to sunrise for her to kneel in front of her rocking chair and discuss all of her concerns with Him. I truly believe that every good thing that has happened to me is a result of her commitment of herself and everything she possessed into the care of the Lord.

# 1

## The Former and the Latter Rains

George alias Jana, Bumble alias Jeremy, and Lassie alias Sox came to our duplex to visit. George and Bumble came to be entertained, and Lassie came to rouse me from sleep at the proper time. She succeeded. That time was in the middle of the night. I believe that the Lord disturbed Lassie in some way so that I would know the following event was not a dream.

George quieted Lassie's barking after she awakened everyone in the house. After a while, everyone seemed to have gone back to sleep again except me. I lay awake in my bed. Suddenly I heard a loud rumble of thunder. Lightning seemed to have hit just outside of our bedroom. However, the sound was not nearly as loud as one would expect in such close proximity to the bolt.

Seconds latter it thundered again and again and again. The sounds came in a pounding rhythm about every four seconds with the same intensity. I began to count, thousand one, thousand two, thousand three, thousand four, BANG. I continued to count and slap the bed on the count of four, and precisely at that instant, there was a quick, short sound of another strike.

This continued to occur six or seven times until, instead of lightning there was the sound of rain as if someone sprayed a water hose across the window. Water streamed a second time across the window, followed by another bolt of lightning, still in the four-second rhythm, followed by a loud BANG. And just as suddenly as it all began, there was silence. Silence filled with wonder.

The following morning it was easy to see that there had been a storm. Many tree limbs were lying about in the yard. The ground was soaked with rain. Nobody that I talked to had experienced anything like the unusual storm I had witnessed. I pondered about the possible meaning for me, but I didn't have a clue.

It was part of my office routine to read my Bible during my coffee break. I had no set pattern as to what I would read from my King James edition. Sometimes I read wherever I happened to open the book. One morning, a few weeks after the storm, I opened the Bible. I began reading Hosea 6:3: "And he shall come to us as the rain, as the latter and the former rains unto the earth."

The passage immediately brought to memory the two rains in the storm that I had experienced, but still nothing of any meaning. I decided to read in the book of Joel. In the second chapter, verse 23, I read: "He will cause to come down for you the rain, the former rain and the latter rain in the last month." I was now convinced that the two similar verses related to the storm. Yet there was nothing to do but keep on searching for the meaning the Lord was trying to show me.

Time passed, and then one evening I was watching television and happened to tune to Rex Humbard. His subject was concerning the former and the latter rains. He had my undivided attention!

He said the former rain was a symbol of the outpouring of the Holy Spirit at Pentecost, and the latter rain was symbolic of the outpouring of the Holy Spirit in the latter days just preceding Jesus' Second Coming. He cited Joel 2:28: "After I have poured out my rains again, I will pour out my Spirit upon all of you! Your sons and daughters will prophesy; your old men will dream dreams, and your young men see visions."

My understanding as to the meaning of the rains was now complete. Years passed during which I experienced many dreams and visions from the Lord.

Mil and I moved from Stillwater to Tulsa. We went to a church meeting at Oral Roberts University Mabee Center to hear Kenneth Copeland, a well known evangelist. When we got there, the arena was packed. The song service was uplifting, but my mind would not settle into the proceedings. I could only think about the many things the Lord had done in my life. Then I began to think only about the two rains.

I wondered why I was not hearing ministers talking about the topic that God had used to impact my life in such a dramatic way. It seemed to be a lost cause for Him to waste such vital information on me when there are so many well-known and articulate ministers available to speak of things important for us to know.

Kenneth Copeland began his message. He said that he had been praying and fasting for forty days. God had given him a new message that he had NOT preached before. The message was about the FORMER AND THE LATTER RAINS!

What is God saying to us? I believe we are living in the latter days just preceding the return of Jesus. The latter rain is a sprinkle now of His Spirit but will be a downpour very soon. We need to use our time wisely in the things that glorify God and witness to those who do not know Jesus as their Lord and Savior.

# 2

# Dream:
## EDUCATION

I had a dream in which I saw an emblem and three words in gold on the face of the book that I held in my left hand. The words were, "THE LIVING BIBLE." Out of the pages from the top of the book began to pour a substance that looked like mashed potatoes.

I ate a bite, then I gave some to a Christian friend, Al, who was seated at an old classroom desk. Behind him was another desk. Seated in it was a state television news-anchor. I told the anchor of an account in which the Lord had shown me His ability to guide me in His supernatural way.

As he arose to leave, he sneered, saying, "We hear stories like that all of the time." His nose immediately grew to about eight inches long, and warts popped out all over it. In a third desk behind the news-anchor sat a stranger. He did not speak to me, and I did not speak to him.

I awoke instantly and was puzzled for a time, for this was such a different dream from anything that I had ever experienced before. I have been told that dreams can originate from one's subconscious or something they have eaten.

At first, nothing came to mind as to its meaning. The dream was unique in that I never had one with such visual detail that ended so abruptly. I began to ponder what the meaning could be. I thought about the substance that we had eaten as it poured from the Bible. At that exact instant just beside our home and far from any rural area, a quail called out during the dead of night.

At that moment, I thought of the connection between the quail and the manna. What looked like mashed potatoes was really manna, God's food, coming from His Word. The story that I told the newsman was true. The growth of his nose represented the attitude of ignorance and indifference to the ways of the Lord. I never fed the stranger any of the manna. He was not to be my concern.

The desks suggested that the dream was about education. The eating of the mania indicated that I would share a new move of God with a selected group of people, such as Al, those who already knew Jesus as their Lord and Savior.

# 3

# Dream:
# GIVE ME THIS MOUNTAIN

The sky was a brilliant blue, as blue as on any postcard I have ever seen. Towering up through the blue was a mountain of red gold rock that cantilevered out over my head.

It appeared to be several thousand feet high. Barely visible were three mountain climbers tied together by a life line. They hung suspended from the bottom of the cantilever and were several hundred yards from the lip of the overhang. Their position on the mountain was IMPOSSIBLE.

The next part of the dream began instantly. My wife, Mil, and I were standing on top of the mountain, and I was looking down at the valley below. I thought, *Mil will be petrified if she looks down with her fear of heights.*

The scene shifted. I saw three people at the foot of the mountain who had just finished their descent. I heard in my spirit, "The woman is a heroine and she has set a new record."

For the final scene, I saw the guide walking toward me. He was dressed like a Swiss mountain climber, yet his clothing was as white as the brightest white I have ever seen. His face was in deep shadow in the bright sunlight so that it was hidden from me, but I knew that it was Jesus. He said to me, "People who climb mountains should not carry loads."

The dream ended as quickly as it started, and I awoke immediately. I thought of the mountain and how impossible it was to climb. Yet with the aid of the guide, my wife and I had accomplished it. I knew Mil and I would do something humanly impossible, and Mil would be noted for something very significant. It was obvious that any hardships we were experiencing were to be laid aside immediately. That was not hard to do.

A few weeks passed, and no one outside of our family knew about the events occurring in my life. The Lord always would silence me, saying that He would tell me when the time had come to share what He had shown me. Finally that time came. One Sunday between Sunday school and the morning worship service, I told a friend about the IMPOSSIBLE DREAM, the three people on the mountain, Mil's fear of heights, coming back to the valley, and then seeing the Lord.

I met my wife and we went into the service. That morning our choir director sang a solo. The song he had chosen to sing was "THE IMPOSSIBLE DREAM." As soon as he finished, the pastor began his message, saying, "There were three people on a mountain...." He went on to relate a story about his wife being caught on a mountainside and her fear of heights.

He ended his sermon by explaining that everyone must come back to the valley at some time after being on a mountaintop. He had paraphrased my dream in proper order. I knew God had confirmed that this was a dream that would have some meaning for me, but only in His time would I understand it.

A short time later, I watched a service conducted by Dr. Robert Schuller on TV. He was talking about what to do when you face a mountain or a problem. He stated that the Lord would lead you around it, over it, tunnel through it, or He would turn it to gold if you would wait on Him. As I was considering these alternatives, I thought of the gold. The Lord touched me and I knew my answer. It was, "Wait and see the mountain turned to gold."

Time elapsed. We found another evangelist on television we enjoyed listening to very much. It was Charles Stanley, pastor of First Baptist Church of Atlanta, Georgia. We listened to him regularly until the time slot was changed on the station. One evening when I returned from work, Mil told me that she found Dr. Stanley on television that day and she had taped the service. She added that she knew that the message by Dr. Stanley was especially for me.

His service began with "Have you ever had a dream in your life? I mean something so big that you wanted to accomplish. A big dream. A big goal. Like a mountain, it stood before you and you wanted to accomplish it so much!"

As Dr. Stanley continued speaking, further excerpts brought me more conformation that the dream I had was of the Lord. Some of his other comments also gave me some direction that the Lord was going to move me in were as follows: "So today, you no longer have that dream. You've given up and settled for a life that God never intended for you.

"But here is a man who had a tremendous dream, a great goal in his life. For forty-five years, Caleb carried his dream, his goal. And now, after forty-five years, he is saying GIVE ME THIS MOUNTAIN!

"The criticism of other people can steal our dreams. `It's too big.' `It's IMPOSSIBLE.'" He went on to relate the story of Caleb and how God had used him mightily to lead His people to victory. God had promised him a mountain, Hebron, for his obedience and because he had wholly followed the Lord.

"If you can delicately handle mole hills in your life, God will trust you with a mountain. You may ask God for a mountain when you realize the absolute necessity of wholly depending upon God.

"Our point of desperation is God's choice, pivotal hub, His point of opportunity to demonstrate how great He is," Dr. Stanley concluded. Mil was right. The message on that tape was tailor made for me. Whenever I got a little depressed, I would listen to the tape again.

It was a great lift to my spirit, until one day the tape broke. I missed it's uplifting message. Doctor Stanley had a monthly magazine called *In Touch* that we received. He featured one of his sermons in it each issue. His ministry also sold tapes of his weekly sermon.

It occurred to me that I could order a tape to replace the broken one, but I didn't know the program number or the long passed date that it had aired. I sent in a request and described the sermon as best I could remember. Several days later I went to the mailbox to get my mail. When I put my hand in the box, I literally felt the Presence of the Lord touch me. I pulled out a package. It was the tape that I had ordered!

I was amazed the staff had found the proper tape with only my very inexact description. In less than a week, the magazine came. On the front cover was a picture of a mighty mountain, and the feature sermon was "Give Me This Mountain."

No wonder the staff had no problem in finding a very old sermon. God's timing in replacing the tape that so lifted me up at very low times was, as always, perfect. The dream that has become such a part of my life occurred during the early morning of December, 24, 1975.

Since that time, God has brought it to my mind in many ways. Usually, it is a reminder that His promises are forever. The mountain has turned into gold after a very long period of waiting, but at a critical time in our lives when Mil and I needed His support. Numerous times this dream has come to my mind and was followed by a minister's talk about some part of Caleb's life.

For instance, one evening in a service in our home church, I had a split-second vision of an opening into the side of a mountain. I pondered about its meaning and decided that it must have been an opening to a gold mine. With this in mind, I wondered if the preacher who was visiting for that service would have Caleb as the center of his talk.

And sure enough, he spoke on Caleb. He stated that he came prepared to preach one of two sermons, and he had not decided which it would be until he had walked on the podium. God knew. God knows the beginning from the end. He knew what the pastor's choice would be before the sermon was even a thought in the minister's mind.

From this experience, I have learned that God already knows every thought that comes to my mind and the decision that I will make before it even occurs to me. This is NOT to say that I do not have complete free will or that I always make the correct decision. Sometimes, I am preoccupied with other things in my life, or lazy, or just want to have my own way in a matter. God, please forgive me for the things I do that do not glorify You.

# 4

# Dream:
## CHRISTMAS GIFT

Shortly after I had been notified that my job at Oklahoma State University had been terminated, the Lord began a new movement in my life. I felt as though I had been placed in a training program precisely fitted to my need for understanding clearly his plan for my future. It was so unique that I am reticent to speak about it. I had never heard of anyone having a similar experience.

I knew of no pastor that I could go to for counsel who had gone through a like occurrence and who could explain any significance for the events which were happening to Mil and me.

God's training program was similar to the "word of knowledge." At times I would have a thought that would remind me of another related thought. Other associated thoughts followed in rapid order until I would come to a word in my mind that was the same as what was originating from some outside source.

That source could be a radio or TV announcer or anyone in my hearing range. The words from the outside source occurred at the exact moment that I thought of it. Within a very few minutes, I would experience a repeat of this circumstance.

This was a confirmation for me to know that that which was occurring was not a coincidence. Even though I was at a complete loss as to any meaning connected with these events, I was at peace in my mind as I recalled some of the experiences of the previous few months.

On one occasion as I was reading Billy Graham's book about angels, an announcer repeated a whole sentence verbatim as I read it. The interesting part about this for me was that I lost my place again and again. I found my place and read the sentence in perfect timing with the speaker as he spoke verbatim the same sentence on the radio program. I learned from that incident that God is doing everything, He is planning for my life with perfect timing.

A short time prior to the dream in this story, this type of experience occurred daily. I began to relax because I knew that God was beginning to give meaning to my thoughts. The words I heard were always the same until Christmas eve arrived. Each time I thought of the word "Christmas," I would hear the word "gift" from some source.

At other times, these words would be reversed. I would think of "gift" and instantly hear "Christmas." I knew in my spirit that Mil and I were going to receive a Christmas gift. I felt like a little child, and I could not wait for the day to arrive. I thought of every possible thing that the gift might be, except, of course, the blessing that He had in store for us.

The dream began instantly, as most of my dreams did. Everything in the dream was clear and in detail to the point that I could see the grain in the wood. I found myself lying in a very old bed covered with a very old patch-work quilt. Above us was a low ceiling in the half lit room.

On the ceiling shined what looked like the beams from three or four flashlights that were moving back and forth like beacons. The light appeared to originate from the foot of our bed. I noticed a glow of light at that source, I sat up and looked down at the floor in that area. I saw a ball of light about three feet in diameter, and in it was a stand to support some type of object.

It was comprised of a piece of oak wood about 3/4' square by 20" high. On the bottom of this shaft were two cross members that formed the base. The object was floating in the air and swinging back and forth in the ball of light. I took the stand in my hand and placed it on the floor. It was at this time that I heard music that was breaking my trend of thought. I looked to see its origin. It came from an antique phonograph player that was next to my side of the bed.

I asked Mil, "Who started this music? I can't understand what is going on."

"I did," she replied. "I thought we should have music at this time."

"I must hear what is being said," I answered.

I reached over and lifted the needle from the record, but it continued to play. Somewhat surprised, I then picked up the record from the player with the tips of my fingers. It still continued to play. I could feel the vibrations caused by the music. Nothing could stop the music.

As I glanced up from the record to the other side of the room, I saw the oak stand that had been in the center of the light. A bright silver box of about 16 inches in each dimension was sitting atop the vertical shaft.

At this moment I heard a voice in my spirit. It said, "In 1899, [*silence*] received a gift of health." The dream ended abruptly and I awoke. It was dawn of Christmas Day. I did not know it yet, but our Christmas gift had just been delivered.

I dressed and went to the living room. Dad was listening to the television, and Beverly Sills was singing "An Old-Fashioned Christmas." This song described the old-fashioned items in the dream. The Lord confirmed to me that the dream related to our present from Him.

I had a gall bladder ailment for a number of years that required medication and a fat-free diet. During that time, Mil had suffered from severe arthritis. The condition of her hip was so painful that she had a problem getting out of bed and the knuckles of her fingers were extremely swollen. Two weeks later we realized that both of these afflictions had slowly disappeared.

Suddenly I realized that our gift was simultaneous healing. I had not known before this time that the Lord heals. My church teachings had never discussed that such a blessing was available for me. I was learning a new truth. The meaning of the dream became clear to me as I thought about its significance.

**The light symbolized Jesus, for He is the Light. Within the Light was the stand for the gift of healing; however, I had to set the stand in place in order to receive His gift. The fact that the music could not be stopped showed that the gift was operating under God's power, not ours.**

The time of silence in the statement regarding the gift was a blank space. The fact that there was no name in that space indicates to me that the gift is not limited to anyone. Anyone who desires may sign his or her name in that space to receive it.

Many times since this revelation, I have witnessed the healing power shown to me in that dream. I have often felt the direction of the Holy Spirit as people have been prayed for, yet the results are often very different. Sometimes instant healing occurs. Other times there is a long period of time before I see an answer, and in other instances, I do not understand the results at all. In Isaiah 55:8, 9, the Lord says,

"This plan of mine is not what you would work out, neither are my thoughts the same as your thoughts! For just as the heavens are higher than the earth, so are my ways higher than yours, and my thoughts than yours."

The distance between the heavens and earth is infinity. How measureless is the mind of God compared to the finite mind of man.

In summary, God sometimes uses the foolish things to confound the wise. The gift that God gave me seemed very foolish in its beginning form, as at first it seemed to serve no apparent purpose. In its final form, it became a type of the "word of knowledge," certainly a gift that does have a Biblical base.

# 5

# Vision:
## Surely Goodness and Mercy

My job at OSU had been terminated, and now I know the reason why the Lord allowed it to happen. I could not have stayed focused on my job while He was showing me so many new things. I had many sleepless hours every night.

My mind was filled with many questions, and yet I knew of no one who could give me the answers. I tried to remember every incident in its chronological order from the night of my first dream concerning my education to the current moment. I learned nothing in this manner, except that the truth of Psalm 139 was becoming more indisputable in every way. God was showing me that he knew when I stood up or sat down.

Despite my lack of understanding of what was happening, He knew where I was in the dark. He knew what I was about to say before I could open my mouth. There was as little order to my life in those days as there is now in my attempt to describe my frustration.

On the night of this first vision, I awoke during the night and began to think about Psalm 23. During high school, I had memorized it in one of my literature classes. Silently I recited,

> "The Lord is my shepherd; I shall not want.
> He maketh me to lie down in green pastures;
> He leadeth me beside still waters.
> He restoreth my soul: he leadeth me in the paths
> Of righteousness for his name's sake.
> Yea, though I walk through the valley of the shadow

*Of death, I will fear no evil: for thou art with me;
Thy rod and thy staff they comfort me.
Thou preparest a table before me in the presence of
Mine enemies: thou anointest my head with oil;
My cup runneth over."*

There was no problem until I came to the last verse. I tried reciting it rapidly, then slowly. I tried every mental gymnastic that I could think of to bring the verse back to my memory. Nothing succeeded. I decided to get up and find my Bible to read the last verse. I had to have some peace of mind if I was going to be able to get back to sleep.

I sat up in bed, and as my feet hit the floor, a home projection screen lit up brightly immediately in front of me. The bright light from its surface illuminated our bedroom.

A small dot appeared in the center of the screen and moved to the center of my forehead. On the screen appeared the word "surely." The lettering, approximately four inches high, was like that in the word just typed. I looked at it until I finally thought "surely." Instantly, the word appeared to be cut up in dozens of pieces. Then it swirled around like water going down a drain and disappeared.

Then came a second dot similar to the first. The word "goodness" followed and stayed on the screen until I thought "Surely goodness." It went down the same drain as the first. A pattern of movement was now established. "And" followed by "mercy" appeared in similar manner. When I said, "Surely goodness and mercy," I suddenly realized that I had been cued to the last verse I hadn't been able to remember. I added, "will follow me all the days of my life and I will dwell in the house of the Lord forever."

At that instant, the screen and the room went dark. The vision was ended. The Presence of God's Spirit was evident to me. I noted the promise in that verse and accepted it as a gift given to me by my Father.

It was later that I found that experiencing these events was His method of preparing me to be an encouragement to people as they walk through dark valleys in their lives. We must remember that "greater is He (the Holy Spirit) that is in us than he that is in the world."

# 6

# Dream:
## STORM, OPPRESSION

The rain was pouring down in the early dawn. As I approached the corner of Duck and Miller from the south, I could see that I would have to detour across the corner of the intersection and head west up the slope on Miller. I was riding in a very small and slow vehicle similar in size to a golf cart.

There was no way I could navigate the flooded streets. When I made the turn, a sinister-looking figure appeared and began walking beside me. He bumped the side of my sluggish cart as I tried to pick up speed to outdistance him up the slope. I lacked the power. When I slowed down, so did he. I could not get away from this oppressive figure.

My only hope was that when I reached level ground, I would have the necessary speed to pull away from him. As I got to that point, the sun began to shine brightly. I arrived at the next intersection and turned right toward the field house. The evil character walked away. I believe it was the light that he could not endure. When I approached the field house, my small vehicle fell apart. I began to try to reassemble my cart. As I did, I heard in my spirit, "Why are you trying to put this back together? You have three new ones over there." My eyes were directed to my father's home on Hall of Fame. At this point, my dream suddenly ended.

During the next few days, I told those with whom I had been sharing my experiences about the storm and the sunshine that followed. I wondered if the dream was prophetic in any way.

The next Sunday morning, Mil and I attended our church service. Charlie, our pastor, began his sermon by saying, "My wife and I have never gone through a big storm, but many have." He added that it is in stormy times that God can most easily show His faithfulness. As He leads us through our problems, we can see His abundant provision for His children. It is also a time when we are more likely to listen, as our daily lives are interrupted from the routines that have dulled our senses.

# 7

# Psychology, Psychiatry: Golf

I didn't know why at the time, but I was completely engrossed in listening to a discussion about psychology and psychiatry. I had never heard in such detail the scope of their respective practices and the difference between the practitioners. And since I was viewing this program as it was aired on a Christian network, the doctor described the further differences between Christian and secular practices when employed from the perspective of each profession.

Since this happened during the time when I was unemployed, I could play golf anytime I felt like it. And I felt like it every day, usually at a time when the other members of our foursome wanted to play. However, the morning following the television program, I decided to get this duty out of the way early. I went to the golf coarse early in the morning, a time that I rarely went. When I got there, I could find only one person with whom to play.

We teed off, and since our balls had been miraculously hit in the same direction, we walked together. My playing partner was a young man, and I assumed that he was enrolled at Oklahoma State University. I was close in my guess, however, he told me that he had just graduated and was preparing to move to his new job to begin practicing psychology. I knew then why I had had a crash course of knowledge in that particular science. As we played the next few holes, I found it easy to talk to him about his chosen field. When I began to converse with him about what I had learned concerning psychology from a Christian perspective, he listened. He said he found this very interesting, but this view was all new to him.

He listened more intently and said even less as I began to share some of the dreams and other encounters that I had experienced. Sometimes I find it most difficult to share my stories with people when there seems to be no response on their part to hear of happenings with which they have had no experience with which to relate. It is at times like this that I try to be very sensitive to their reactions. I do not want to overstate anything that would put a conversation block between us.

It was when we teed off across the creek on number thirteen that this young graduate turned to me and said, "You sure have a lot of faith, don't you?"

"This is not faith at all. It would be faith only if it were only based on my beliefs. What I am telling you is based on facts," I answered.

He said, "I believe you. I have felt for a long time that there was something in my understanding of life that was missing. I am sure that this is it. Thank you for sharing your stories with me."

I saw this golfer one more time at a distance. I have wondered many times where he is and what he is doing. I am sure a seed of some kind was planted in that young man's thought the morning we played golf together, but I wonder if anyone ever watered it.

It is when I look back that I see clearly all that God has done. I know beyond any doubt that God changed my tee-off time in order to show that young man the fairway to the eternal.

# 8

## AM I IN YOUR WILL?

Each one of us is unique in God's sight because we are different from each other in many ways. We differ in knowledge, gifts, talents, desires, emotions, and commitment to the challenges that face us daily. Knowing this, I continually ask myself if I am making the choices in my own unique life that glorifies God, especially during periods of loneliness.

When I sense that God is directing my way, I am mentally very comfortable. But when I feel that I have been making bad decisions, the opposite is true. I realize that feeling is coming from my emotions and therefore not to be trusted. However, it is a real feeling that I have to deal with.

My answer to this problem when it arose was to get my golf clubs, go to a practice field, hit balls, and pick them up. This pleasant exercise restored my sense of well-being.

It was a very dark, cloudy fall day. The clouds hung low in the sky and were tumbling swiftly southward. My mood was as gloomy as the somber weather. Nothing seemed to be going right in my mind. I was convinced that God had abandoned me. For a moment, I challenged Him. I thought, *God, if I am in your will, make the sun shine*. In the next moment, I felt guilt for having had such a thought. However, I could not help looking up. The clouds did not split open, but they thinned out and began to move around one point so that I could see through the opening that appeared. Through the opening I saw the peak of a giant thunderhead thrusting up through the deep blue sky above.

Seconds later that peak began to split open from the top in a downward direction UNTIL in the center of that opening appeared the SUN. The field surrounding me was flooded by its brilliant rays. God had answered me in a most humbling way.

This incident was so simple in one way but yet speaks volumes to me each time I recall that extraordinary day. Those two openings were aligned so that the sun shone only in the area where I was standing. After a few seconds, the clouds closed together. The sun did not shine again that day. God grows larger in my mind each time I grasp another truth inherent in that display of His power.

# 9

# Charismatic:
## Worried About Her Husband

During the early days of my redirected walk with the Lord, I was very shy about sharing my experiences except with those who were very close to me. In time, I became more bold in my witness. This brought about a new understanding of a reality that bothered me deeply.

Many Christians are so deeply rooted in their beliefs that they will not receive anything that differs in the least with their own church traditions. I lost friends by speaking about the revelations as I experienced them. I wondered why God was allowing this to happen to me when nothing that I said was untrue. This is still somewhat of a mystery, of which I only have an opinion.

As I played a round of golf with, I thought, a friend and fellow member of my church, I told him of the dreams and the other events that were happening daily in my life. I had no idea how he was receiving my conversation until we were about to leave the course.

He said to me something to the effect, "Bill, I am a dispensationalist. I don't believe that God acts the way you have spoken in this present dispensation. You've gone charismatic."

He left for home and I stood there stunned by his reaction. Nothing that I had told him was untrue. I didn't even know what a dispensationalist or a charismatic was at that time. How could my discourse that I meant for encouragement have been received so critically. I really questioned the Lord at that moment.

"WHY?" I felt so stupid and depressed that I had opened my mouth. I wanted a hole to hide in.

Shortly after this put-down, Mil received a call from our pastor. She told me he had asked her to come to his office. He said that he wanted to talk to her about some service for the church. She left me at home and was gone for a short time. After she left for the appointment, I wondered what that service could be. At that moment I heard, "He's worried about her husband."

It wasn't hard to surmise the sequence of events. My golfing friend had visited with the pastor, and now the pastor was calling Mil to discuss the incident. It really didn't bother me at all. In fact, I found it humorous. God had shown me that he knew about the problem, so I decided to leave the solution in His capable hands.

When Mil returned home, I asked her what had transpired. She said, "Charlie wanted to talk about some items of church work."

I laughed and replied, "Yes, and I know what one of the items is—ME. Isn't that right?"

"That's right. Your friend talked to Charlie about you and his concerns about the things that you claimed are occurring in your life. Charlie told him that he himself didn't have a problem with anything that you are saying or doing. He said it is not Satan's purpose to build one's faith in God by doing the wonderful things that have been happening in your life. He also said he has seen your faith growing every day. Charlie told me not to be concerned either with anything that has happened. He wasn't going to be."

I lost a friend, and I don't know why it happened under the circumstances. It certainly wasn't my choice in any way. I have given this much thought. Maybe, just maybe, our society is becoming less and less able to recognize the power of God and the way He speaks to His people.

We assign the miracles that Jesus performed to the age of His life on earth. Thereby, the Holy Spirit is limited in working fully in our present age. He could do so much more if we would only recognize and thank Him for his awe-inspiring deeds. God never changes, but we sure have.

# 10

# Job:
## Vet Medicine Hospital

Ten years of employment in the office of Oklahoma State University architect's office were over, I believed. This was a division of the school physical plant. I began working at the university in 1966, when the campus building program was expanding in every direction.

In 1975 the program was nearing completion, and the need for my services as an architectural designer was over. There was one large project remaining to be constructed, the Veterinary Medicine Hospital, but it was scheduled to be designed by an off-campus architectural firm.

Immediately following my departure, the Presence of the Lord intensified into a rain of God's power in my life. The gift of a word of knowledge occurred several times each day, always unexpectedly. My education in some of the ways of the Lord kept my mind riveted on the experiences that were happening.

I felt for a while that I had been isolated from the world that I had known for fifty-four years. During this new adjustment, I had complete peace of mind, but I had no idea as to the direction that Mil and I were being led. There was really nothing to do but wait for the Lord to direct our steps.

Our daughter, Joyce, had moved to the Kansas City area to begin her teaching career. Mil and I decided to visit her for a while. In the two days preceding our departure, I heard "OSU" five times as I thought about my next job, and the day we were leaving, I heard "vet medicine hospital" twice as I thought of OSU.

I was convinced that this would be my next employment, even though I had been told words to the contrary by the administrators of the campus physical plant.

As we were leaving my mother's home, I gave Joyce's phone number to her and told her that the university would be calling her for the number someday to reach me. We would return then to work on the hospital. I know she was glad to hear that we would be returning to Stillwater, but I could tell that she questioned my sanity.

Weeks went by while we were in Kansas City. The newspapers in that area printed nothing about the building program on the campus of Oklahoma State University in Stillwater, Oklahoma of course. During this stay with Joyce, I was having a new dream every third night over a period of two or three weeks.

If I had had any idea that the Lord was going to take such an active role in my life, I would have kept a diary. One dream was about watercolors, so I began working at that as a hobby. This kept me occupied and served as a source of income in a later period of our lives when our finances were becoming exhausted.

I do not remember how many weeks or months we stayed with Joyce, but I missed being steadily employed very much. One morning I was thinking about what God had said to me on the day that we had left Stillwater. I wondered when I would hear from the university.

At that instant, I heard the Lord say, "Meeting to-day." That word from the Lord brought me much needed hope. The following morning I was thinking again about the meeting of the previous day when I heard the Lord say, "There will be a call today."

Now my hopes soared until five o'clock that afternoon. I then knew that the office was closed, and there was no hope of receiving a phone call on that day. I wondered why I had been confused by what I had heard that very morning. I dismissed all thought from my mind about my perplexity and became occupied doing other things.

About nine o'clock that evening, the phone rang. Joyce answered it. She said, "Dad, its long-distance for you."

I knew instantly who was calling. Five o'clock had meant nothing to the Lord. The statement that He had made to me earlier in the day was now confirmed. As I answered, Bill, my former boss, and I exchanged the usual conversation that people have after a period of not having talked with each other. He said that he had been trying to call me earlier in the day, but he had been unable to get my phone number. He said my parents had been out of town and had just returned home that evening.

Then he said, "Bill, we have decided to design the hospital in this office after all. Would you want to work on it?"

I had known for weeks that question would come someday, but I was still not prepared emotionally to answer immediately. I was choked up by the passion of the moment. I had never before experienced anything that compared with this revelation of the Lord's knowledge and control of the future.

After I replied that I would like very much to work on the project, Bill asked when we would be able to return. The office wanted to begin design of the building as soon as possible. I didn't tell him that we were already packed.

The following morning, Mil and I finished our last-minute packing and prepared to get in the car. Mil became very ill during the night. Her equilibrium was so impaired that she was almost unable to walk. I sat down and wondered about what our next move should be.

Should I call the office in Stillwater and delay our return, or should I just wait until afternoon before making a decision? With that thought in my mind, I heard in my spirit, "Get Mil in the car and leave." I went into the room where Mil was resting and said, "Get up and get in the car. We're leaving for home." As we drove away, I asked the Lord to touch her. We had driven only a few miles when she asked me to stop at the next restaurant. She said that she was starving. She was completely well.

I know that Satan had done his best to stop us from returning to the job that the Lord had promised us. Another thought to ponder was God's faithfulness regarding the phone call. By five o'clock, I had given up of ever receiving a call. My faith had been wiped out, but God answered me anyway. When God makes a promise to us, the promise will be kept, for it is based on His character, not on our faith or actions.

# 11

# Dream:
## Gift, Proposal, Readiness

This dream was one of a series that occurred while Mil and I were spending some time in Kansas City with our daughter, Joyce. Most of these dreams dealt with a coming event.

As I look back now at the events of that period, I can see that our having been moved away from Stillwater was probably the only way God could have gotten my complete attention. There was nothing else to do, no one to share with who had gone down a similar path.

In the opening scene of this dream I was looking at a can of candy I had received as a gift. The description on the side said that the candy was made from a very old recipe. The recipe was discovered accidentally when some different kinds of candy were spilled together.

In the next scene, Mil and I saw Joyce passing by in front of us. She suddenly stopped and faced us as a bright light illuminated the back of her hair. She smiled at us broadly, obviously very happy. Mil turned to me and said, "She is preparing for a proposal of marriage."

I responded, "I wonder who is going to do the proposing?"

Scene three followed. A boy between eight and ten years of age stood before me. He was dressed like one of the early militia men of the eighteenth century. He was a Minute Man, and his hair was parted down the middle. Somebody was standing beside him, but I did not know who it was. I said to this person that the next time that this young man goes to the barber, I want to take him.

I awoke instantly as I always did with the end of each dream. Like the others I had had, this dream was as clear as if it had happened in daily life.

It wasn't very long before I understood the meaning of the first scene. The gift I received, symbolized by that can of candy, was a gift made up of many gifts, the gift of praying for the sick, the gift of a word of knowledge, and any other gift as it is needed for a particular situation.

Several years transpired, and one day I was walking down the mall area in downtown Tulsa. Across the way, I saw a large photograph in a window display that looked like the picture of Joyce in my dream. Her hair was backlighted exactly as in the dream. It was not Joyce, but it made me think about the message of proposal for her. A few days later that dream came true, and a short time later, she married Ron. Scene two of the dream had been completed.

I believe scene three relates to our present days. The motto of the Minute Men was preparation for action at a minute's notice. That young man is grown now. It is vital that we are prepared to act at the Lord's direction at a minute's notice.

# 12

# Dream:
## HAPPY DAYS, THE PRESENCE

Days were dragging by slowly in Kansas City as we waited for the time until the design of the Vet Medicine Hospital at OSU would begin. The Lord and I were the only ones who knew that project would be my next job. There was no way for me to know its current status while living at such a distance from Stillwater. It was during this period of Mil's and my life that I was having dreams and confirmations of the dreams, but none of those dealt with our daily activities. This dream remedied that situation.

A young man with bright red hair appeared suddenly before me. He was wearing a jacket that had a checkerboard pattern of three-inch squares. The colors alternated in blue and white. The man stepped toward me, smiled broadly, and then disappeared.

Then I saw a watercolor painting sitting on the seat of a chair and propped against it's back. The picture was of a floral design in black and white. It contrasted sharply with the bright color of the young man's attire.

I awoke instantly and began to think about the young person in the dream. I knew that he was someone that I knew, but who? The smile identified the character, and suddenly my memory was jogged. It was the character "Ralph" in the sit-com *Happy Days*. The next thought was, why him?

Then I wondered if the real focus of the dream was the title *Happy Days*. With that thought, I felt a presence. It began at my feet, continued up the length of my body, and passed over my head. A few seconds later this same sensation was repeated. (This was the first time that I experienced this presence which has occured countless time since.)

The red, white, and blue was so prevalent that I surmised that it must relate in some way to our country. I had not done any painting since I had done some architectural illustrations in years past, so this dream served as an inspiration to begin painting again.

I am including this story even though I do not understand its' meaning. The figure and objects in the dream were as vivid in color and defined in detail as any that I have experienced. I believe God, in His wisdom, has a purpose that He will reveal to me at some future time. Meanwhile, this experience remains as a source of hope as I look forward to that date when God reveals more of His sovereign plan for my life.

# 13

# Protection: Wasps

I was no longer employed at the Oklahoma State University architect's office, and the Lord had told me that my next job would come as a surprise. I didn't know how to find a surprise, so my wife, Mil, and I decided to go on a short vacation.

We went to my grandmother's old farmhouse located in Missouri's Ozark Mountains. The house had been unoccupied for a number of years. Our family used it periodically as a vacation retreat. It was about a four and half hour trip from our home in Stillwater to the farm.

We arrived in the late afternoon, and Mil followed our usual routine on arrival. As she unlocked the house and aired it out, I went around to the well house to turn on the water pump, since water was the top priority item upon arrival. The pump was enclosed in a small house that was about seven feet square.

There was a door on the east side but no windows, so it was very dark inside. On the wall opposite the door, there was an electrical switch that could be reached by stepping over the pump in the center of the structure. When I opened the door, I was greeted by dozens of red wasps. I jumped back, not knowing what to do?

I went around the house and told Mil of our big dilemma. We stood on the porch that extended across the front of the house and thought about our options. We had to have water. We could not stay there without it. It was a long drive back to Stillwater, and we did not want to rent a motel room.

*Maybe I can burn the rascals out*, I thought. But without any water I could set the place on fire. Perhaps some type of insect repellent might work, but I didn't know where I could purchase any. Then I had a most improbable thought. I recalled the time when I had opened the Bible at random to the story concerning the former and the latter rains. We decided to see if God would direct us through His Word.

I got our Living Bible and held it between my hands. It opened slowly, and I glanced down and began to read, "I will protect and bless him constantly and surround him with my love."

That was not an answer that I found acceptable. It was not at all what I had expected if the Lord was speaking. I told Mil that if I walked into that well house, I might get really stung.

The promise of protection was in that scripture, but my fear seemed to cancel it as being a solution to our immediate problem. I entertained this line of thought a little longer. Then I began to consider the fact that if I didn't pursue this course of action, I would always wonder what would have happened. I would question if God really ever spoke to people in this way.

I decided that I had no other option but to go and see if the Lord really had his hand in this or if I was letting my imagination work overtime. Hopefully, I reasoned, I wouldn't get stung over four or five times. As you see, my faith was soaring! I knew God was well pleased with my logic.

Mil informed me that she was going into the house and was not volunteering to take my place. She put herself in position to watch the excitement that was sure to come. I went to the door of the well house and did not dare to think about any consequences of my decision.

I stepped over the pump into the dark room, reached for the switch, and jerked it closed. I stepped over the pump again and to the outside of that wasp nest. I felt only one wasp brush my hair. As I walked away a few feet, I raised my arms and said, "Praise the Lord."

I had never meant it more than I did at that moment. I asked Mil what she had seen. She said, "The wasps circled around you as though you were a pole, but I never saw one land."

As I left the scene, I thought, *Maybe they didn't sting me because I wasn't afraid.* But that was a lie, I was petrified. And then I heard something say in my spirit, "You had better not tell this story to anyone. No one will ever believe you." Well, that was possible, but that was not my most immediate problem.

A few days later, I heard the Lord say that it was time to go home and to attend Sunday school the following weekend. We had not been attending for some time, and I think that He knew that too.

As we packed to leave, I was praying that the wasps would already have left, but they hadn't. In fact, it seemed they had company. As I entered, at the head of the door just inside was a nest of yellowjackets right beside my head. I did not hesitate, I went in. If God had protected me before, then he would do it again.

After I turned off the power, I stepped over the pump and was about to go through the door when the sun from the east caught my hand with its rays. At that moment, a wasp landed on my forefinger.

It folded its wings, rolled over, and fell on the floor at my feet. Then it took off for parts unknown across my grandmother's old garden. The last I saw it, it was flying away from me in a straight line.

God had just confirmed to me the truth of His Word regarding His protection of me. No incidence in all of my life has ever spoken to me more than this one. I began to wonder where the scripture was found that I had read about protection.

It was Psalm 89:24. I learned that it was part of a covenant that God made with David. In this covenant, God assured David that he would always have an heir, but God gave him a warning: "If your children forsake my laws and don't obey them, then I will punish them, but I will never completely take away my lovingkindness from them, nor let my promise fail."

As I wondered how much of that covenant applied to me, I heard the Lord say, "All of it."

# 14

# Heresy:
## Change churches

This is a difficult story to write because it involves the pastor of a mainline church whose views did not reflect the basic tenets of his denomination. I am not going to give facts that could identify this church because I do not wish to embarrass anyone. I write this as a warning that we must not arbitrarily interpret God's Word to correspond with our own humanistic views for any reason.

A fellow employee and a good friend in the firm in which I was working told me of a very troubling concern. Her minister was preaching things that she didn't believe were in line with God's Word.

I had listened to this pastor's radio broadcast, and I had heard him express ideas that were counter to my spirit also. My co-worker's concerns confirmed that I wasn't misunderstanding the message he was delivering.

He claimed that the death of Jesus on the cross was a mistake because God's love is too great to allow that to happen to anyone, much less His own Son. He did not mention that Jesus gave up His own life as a payment for our sins. For me, he completely destroyed the meaning of the cross.

My friend informed me that she was an usher in the church and that she enjoyed her role very much. She felt also that if she changed churches, she would also lose the fellowship of many friends she valued greatly. Her question was, "Shall I change churches or should I try to change things?" That was a good question.

I told that I did not know the answer. We decided that the only true answer would have to come from the Lord, so we decided to pray for direction for her.

About two months later, she received her answer. A girl friend from another city, whom she had not seen for sometime, walked into her office one day. This lady related that for the preceding two days, she felt the Lord had given her a word of knowledge to give to my friend. She had left her home to go shopping for groceries, but instead she had driven from her home to Stillwater to see her friend and deliver God's message.

It was, "Change churches." Obviously this was a true word from the Lord, for she was completely unaware of her friend's request for direction concerning her situation. This is not so mysterious when we understand the awesome power of the same Holy Spirit who is present in all of God's children who are seeking after Him.

We need to understand 1 Peter 2:15, "It is God's will that your good lives should silence those who foolishly condemn the Gospel without knowing what it can do for them, having never experienced its power."

I do not believe my friend's pastor could ever have made such an erroneous statement if he had experienced that power of the Gospel. He was actually condemning Christ's death on the cross as being of no value for our salvation.

Obviously he did not understand the horrific price Jesus has paid for us or the true meaning of love. *"Greater love has no man, than he should lay down his own life for a friend."*

# 15

# Nursing Home:
## Last Chance

    God can use the worst of times in one's life for His glory. This certainly happened in Mil's and my life. I was out of work, and though the Lord had told me that my next job would come as a surprise, this was not a valid excuse in today's society for at least not appearing to be actively seeking employment.
    I interviewed for work as an architectural designer, and each time that I believed I was about to be hired, the employer would decide to delay my hiring until they had more building projects. It was a frustrating time for me. In my previous thirty-five years of employment, I hadn't been out of work for any period of time.
    Mil also looked for work and found employment as a nurse's aide in a nursing home. As we look back now, it was a time when God showed us personally that He was working all things for His good.
    Mil's shift was on duty from about three o'clock in the afternoon until eleven in the evening. Mil not only ministered to the physical needs of the patients, she also encouraged them in every way she could. She became acquainted with Gwen, who had come to the home with a broken hip.
    Mil spent much time with Gwen and her roommate, conversing with the two patients. Gwen's roommate refused any encouragement, while Gwen listened to Mil but usually remained silent.
    When Gwen's husband also broke his hip, the two were moved into another room. After a period of time, the husband recovered enough to go at times to a lounge area by himself.

One evening Mil and the aide who was working with her were putting Gwen to bed. More supplies were needed for Gwen's comfort, so the other aide left to go after them. This was Mil's opportunity to talk privately about Gwen's spiritual need. She asked her, "Gwen, do you know Jesus as your Lord and Savior?"

She answered, "No, I don't think so."

"Would you like to know him?"

"Yes," she replied.

"Then pray after me. Speak up and tell the Lord that you want Him to come into your life. As you pray with me, you will be telling the world that you are accepting Jesus as your Savior. He said that anyone who comes to Him will have Him as their personal advocate before God. But anyone who denies Him as their Lord and Savior, He will deny before the Father."

Gwen prayed in a very clear voice to accept Jesus as her Lord and Savior. The other aide then returned to the room, and Gwen was settled for the evening. Mil told her that she would return to read to her after her shift was over.

Mil returned and read to her the fourteenth chapter of the book of John, which begins, "Let not your heart be troubled. You are trusting God, now trust in me. There are many homes up there where my Father lives, and I am going to prepare them for your coming. When everything is ready, then I will come and get you, so that you can always be with me where I am. If this weren't so, I would tell you plainly. And you know where I am going and how to get there."

When Mil returned the next afternoon, she went to the office to get her day's work schedule. It was then that she was told that Gwen had left during the night to be with her new Lord and Savior. I believe that God had given Gwen one last chance to be with Him eternally.

# 16

# Dream:
## Rod's Coincidence

During the final days of my employment at OSU, I saw many signs and experienced many wonders. I often shared them with my friend Al, who God used to bring me to an awareness of the Bible's prophecy concerning the days prior to Christ's Second Coming.

My hope was that he could continue to help me in ascertaining the reason for the new direction my life had taken. Rod was a student draftsman who was an employee whose salary was on an hourly bases. He set his own work schedule.

One day Rod overheard one of the conversations between Al and me. Apparently the subject matter we had been talking about had aroused his curiosity. He asked me to tell him about some incidents I had shared with Al. I agreed and spoke with him during a coffee-break. I related a few of the events that I had witnessed in the past few weeks.

Each story I told him about, he perceived to be only a coincidence. He said that he had similar experiences all the time. I assured him that I was not trying to convince him of anything. I had nothing to sell or promote.

That evening I was watching a television program called "Wild Kingdom." The theme of the program was "Deadly Snakes of India." I was impressed with the courage of the snake hunters as they pulled highly poisonous snakes from their dens. But after watching the same routine over and over, my interest began to wane.

My Bible was lying beside me, so I picked it up and began to read at the point at which it opened. It was Acts 28:31. "As Paul gathered an armful of sticks to lay on the fire, a poisonous snake, driven out by the heat, fastened itself onto his hand!"

I was very surprised at the parallel of the television program to the story in the Bible. Mil was in the kitchen preparing our evening meal. I related to her the "coincidence." I told her that I was going to open the Bible again and see what would happen. When I opened the Bible again, I began to read the verse on which my eyes fell. It was, "Their talk is foul and filthy like the stench from an open grave. Their tongues are loaded with lies. Everything they say has in it the sting and poison of deadly snakes" (Romans 3:13).

I had no idea how the Lord had accomplished that feat, but I knew that it was not a coincidence. It made me realize that the power of God is so far beyond my limited knowledge that I was overpowered mentally.

When I arrived at the office the following morning, the only person who had arrived before me was Rod. I started to pass by him and proceed to my office. However, I made the decision to tell him about the coincidence of the night before.

I related to him the incident as it happened. He went rigid, and his face turned bright red. He said nothing for several seconds. I wondered what it was that I had said that affected him so radically. Finally, he looked up from his drafting board, turned to me, and said, "I suppose that I will have to tell you. I had a dream this morning just before I got up. I dreamed that I reached down to the ground. When I did, a snake ran up my arm. I grabbed it by the tail and threw it. Its head flew off."

I thought about his story for a moment. I decided to have some obvious fun. I said, "Rod, that is a real coincidence isn't it?"

"No, no it wasn't a coincidence."

Several weeks later, Rod again overheard a conversation between Al and me. We were talking about a personal problem that one of us had.

He said, "Do you know what I do when I am faced with a problem like that? I pray about it."

I was amazed at the change in Rod's life after his dream. The God of coincidence had now become the God of his personal life.

Why doesn't God intervene in all circumstances when I try to witness for Him? I don't know. However, I really like the concept. This is the only time that He ever spoke to a dissenter of mine in such a powerful way. I really was elated with His resolution in this instance.

I suppose that if He did this in every instance, I would become an individual filled with pride in having such a gift. The idea of how I might abuse this power is very scary, especially to me. I think God did this incident ONE TIME in order to show me His power to redirect a person's life in a manner that suits His will and not my ego.

# 17

# Deacon:
# HUMOR, SEMINAR

During the time I was unemployed, I learned many new facts. I discovered that the Lord was speaking the same message to many pastors at the same time. Usually for periods of a month to six weeks, when I listened to my radio tuned to Christian stations, this fact became very apparent.

I recall most vividly a time when it seemed that the story about Hezekiah was the only story in the Bible. Other similar themes came and went quickly in the same manner. I knew this was occurring, for I had little to do but listen to the radio. The Lord's theme when this story happened was Proverbs, chapter 31.

Revival was a reality in our church. Charlie, our new pastor, had come to Stillwater about the same time God had enrolled me in His reeducation program. Our church services had grown from one eleven o'clock service to three meetings to handle the growth we were experiencing.

The eleven o'clock service was designated for the townspeople, ten o'clock service for the college students, and eight-thirty for church members who had been associated with the ministry for a number of years.

Mil and I were attending the early service, which was very informal. One of the deacons was appointed to select members to act as ushers and to take up the offering. This deacon assigned the duties in the foyer as the participants arrived. Two aspects of this story were occurring simultaneously.

The first dealt with the death of a well-known pastor. It was a topic on an evening television program. His passing was totally unexpected, so much that a minister friend of his, who conducted the funeral service, used as his text Isaiah 55:8.

"This plan of mine is not what you would work out, neither are my thoughts the same as yours! For just as the heavens are higher than the earth, so are my ways higher than yours, and my thoughts than yours."

At the time, Mil was working at a nursing home. When I picked her up, I related this story to her. I said, "I have never read this scripture before, that I recall, but it sure seems to fit the position that we are in now."

The following morning was a Sunday. When we arrived in the foyer, the deacon in charge of selecting the group to take up the offering picked me to assist in that service. When we came to the altar, a Bible was lying open in front of me. I began to read, "This plan of mine is not what you would work out." This was part of the scripture I had spoken to Mil about the previous evening. This was confirmation to me that this was God's personal word for us. Than a second thought came to me. *Who opens this Bible and is it reopened every week?*

Sometime during the following week, I heard the Lord say to me in my spirit, *You are going to take up the offering next Sunday.*

At this point, my curiosity took over, and I was more than willing to help take the offering again. I told Mil about the word from the Lord, and I added, "I wonder what He would do if we came about fifteen minutes late?" I knew that everyone who would have a part in the service would have been selected by that time.

Sunday morning arrived and we left for church fifteen minutes late. I was wondering how God was going to handle this situation. I knew it was no problem for Him, but I was just curious. I took off my coat upon arrival at church, hung it up, and turned around only to face the deacon in charge. He was taking his coat off as he stood behind me. He was fifteen minutes late also. I was the first person picked for duty that morning.

I had a plan but God had a much better one. Don't tell me that our Father doesn't have a keen sense of humor. Nothing ever has struck me as being funnier than that moment. I had been had!

God was not through with me that morning either. When I went to the altar, the Bible was open to the 31st chapter of Proverbs. This was the second aspect of this story. It was the same chapter God had kept before me. That answered another question about who was in charge of opening the Bible.

Years passed, and Mil and I were now members of a church in Tulsa. The church was conducting a weekend seminar. The membership was divided into small groups for a topic of discussion to be provided at the beginning of the sessions. The theme of each meeting was not given in advance so that all thoughts would be spontaneous.

We shared our hopes and concerns with one another. One lady from another denomination said she really wanted to be a member of our church. However, she had a problem with being baptized again. She felt as if that would say her first baptism hadn't counted. I understood her dilemma, and confessed that I too had felt a certain stiffness in the church at times. I had visited other churches where men had hugged each other in Christian fellowship.

The meeting ended and we joined all of the other groups in a joint session. Someone in the group commented about the seemly lack of fellowship among the male members. With this statement, the embracing began and the stiffness barrier was broken.

Mil and I arrived a little early the next morning to attend our small-group meetings. The woman who had expressed her concern about the baptism rite had arrived before me. We began talking about her enigma. I suggested to her that she might be taking this distress a little too seriously. I recounted some of my past experiences with the Lord and particularly the humor of the story about taking up the offering.

I told her, "Remember, God is the author of humor, certainly not Satan. I don't believe that He wants this predicament to destroy your joy in not becoming a member here if it is your wish." At this moment, the leader and the other members of our morning assemblage entered the room.

Our leader announced the subject for our discussion—"God's sense of humor." I saw the lady glance at me when the subject was announced.

God's sovereign plan was certainly not one that I would ever have worked out. There were years separating the two incidents. Never could I have ever had the foresight to use the humor of the first incident in such unique way to show the lady that He was concerned about anything that concerned her. God does work in mysterious ways His wonders to perform.

# 18

# Job:
## Wait, Surprise

My work on the Veterinary Medicine Hospital was very near completion. I heard in my spirit that it was time for me to resign. I was not to wait until my job was terminated by the management. At the same time, I heard that my next employment would come as a "surprise," so I resigned immediately.

How do you look for a "surprise"? By its very definition, you really can't. I was concerned that false expectations would take control over my better judgment. I wanted to talk to a knowledgeable counselor who had previously experienced situations that were similar to mine, but I found no one. I had to make my decision with fear and trembling.

I knew in my spirit that I should wait on the Lord to direct me regarding my next employment. This way of finding a new job completely contradicted the prevalent viewpoint of society regarding direction. I knew if I did nothing, I would be viewed by others as lazy, misguided, and confused by my overactive imagination.

None of this was true, but I had nothing to show as evidence for my decision. I wondered why God had let me get into such a predicament. As the days went by, I decided to look for work periodically to satisfy my critics while I waited for the situation to develop.

I did come close to finding employment in Oklahoma City. An architectural firm was very interested in hiring me, but since new construction was very slow, they decided at the last moment to delay hiring me until their work load increased.

Waiting was not too difficult until Mil and I begin to run short of finances. We were living in a leased house in Stillwater, and our landlord wanted to know if we planned to re-lease our home for another year. I understood his concern, but I did not have the slightest idea of when or from where my "surprise" was coming. I had only a few days until I had to have an answer. With each passing day, the mental pressure continued to grow. I wondered what course of action I would take if I heard nothing from the Lord.

I thought of a possibility, and decided to talk to our pastor, Charlie, through whom the Lord had spoken to me many times. I made an appointment for the following week. Now all that I had to do was to decide what I wanted to talk about. I could think of no subject for discussion except getting his "perspective" concerning my current decisions.

My mother was in the hospital at this time with a broken hip, so Mil and I went to visit her. When we arrived, my father and a deacon from our church were in the room with her. We settled into a general conversation as we passed the time.

Our discourse turned to our impressions of Charlie and our observations concerning the growth of church attendance since he had become our pastor. The deacon said that what impressed him the most was Charlie's "perspective" of life's order. At that instant, I knew I had heard the Lord, and I knew what the topic of conversation with the pastor would be when we met.

When the day came for our meeting, Charlie and I began our conference reminiscing about past experiences. I told him about my present problem and my desire to get his perspective pertaining to my decisions. Charlie exclaimed that he had forgotten something. Getting up, he quickly went to his secretary's office. While he was there, he placed a call, talked for few moments, and then returned.

"I just recalled that I had a conversation with an architectural firm in Tulsa a couple of months ago. I had forgotten that they had told me of an opening on their staff for a designer. I just called their office, and the job is still open. Bill, I just set up an interview for you."

I was positive that this was an answer regarding the surprise the Lord had for me. When I went for the job interview in Tulsa, it did not go well. There were many questions concerning my character, did I have a drinking problem, and other questions relating to my integrity.

They questioned my ability to serve as an architectural designer. I left filled with doubt that I could fit into their corporate system. I knew that I could do the work required if I had the opportunity, but I did not know if I could survive in that kind of environment until I could prove my value to them.

As I returned home, I was very frustrated with how the interview had gone. In fact, the more I thought about it, the angrier I became over the whole affair. The next day as Mil and I were sitting in the Sunday morning church service, I was still fuming and intensely angry. My attitude seemed inappropriate and certainly not very spiritual for someone who had come to worship the Lord.

Charlie began his sermon with the statement, "Sometimes the Lord has to make a person very angry in order to get them to move. There is such a thing as righteous anger." I elbowed Mil gently and whispered, "We are moving to Tulsa."

I called the office in Tulsa the next morning. They offered to hire me if I wanted to come. We agreed on a salary and Mil and I prepared to move to Tulsa and take the job that was definitely a "surprise."

The reason the job had not been filled previously was because the firm already had a particular individual in mind to fill the position. However, for several months, the person had declined to accept the position. As soon as we had moved to Tulsa, this party reconsidered the company's offer and called to take the position.

He got the design post shortly after I arrived, but not until after the Lord had moved us to the city where He wanted us to reside. To continue in this office, I had to learn a new discipline in the field of architecture.

I did learn from this experience that I was still capable of being reeducated at fifty-five years of age. I was one of the first to experience what is now known in the business world as "down sizing." If you are passing through such a valley, be aware that God has a place and a purpose where you fit.

# 19

# Vision:
## WATERCOLOR

There were years between this vision and my understanding of the message it proclaimed. I was painting occasionally, and I already had a dream concerning watercolors. The Lord acts in my life in very unusual ways at the most unusual times. He always gets my attention.

I arrived home in the late afternoon from work. The sun was setting, and my energy level was about equal to the fading light of the hour. Mil was busy in the kitchen preparing our meal, so I went on into our bedroom to rest for a few moments. I lay on my back in the dim-lighted room and gazed at the ceiling.

A very short time later, a picture was projected on the ceiling above me. It was a beautiful watercolor about two and a half feet high by four feet long. It was the picture of a barn in the early morning sunrise. Streaks of gold and white were on the gray siding on the front face of the barn. There were also patches of the same color on the ground below.

The rolling terrain around the structure was very striking. The painting was one of the most interesting and yet simple ones I have ever seen. All of the details were very sharp and clearly defined. The projector of the color slide seemed to be located at my side. It continued to shine for possibly a minute or more, then turned off.

Emotionally, the experience did not affect me at all. Outside of admiration for the brilliant colors, my mind was almost blank. I wondered what the message of the vision might be. At the time I had no idea as to its particular meaning.

A few seconds elapsed, and then the projector came on again and displayed the same slide. Now the Lord had my attention. I began to memorize every detail and shape in the work. I looked at every individual fence post and the edges of the roof overhang.

The difference in value between the metal roof and the sky gave depth to the landscape. This time the projector stayed on for a considerable period of time until I was sure that I had all of the pertinent information with which to reproduce the watercolor. At the instant that I thought I had everything committed to memory, the screen went dark.

The next day I made a pencil sketch in my sketch book of the vision. Several weeks later, I painted a watercolor of the drawing because I was afraid I would forget the unique coloring. When I was finished, I thought I had done a good job of reproducing it, but the satisfaction that usually came with finishing a new creation never came.

I kept the painting around the house for a few months until one day I finally decided to give it away. I packaged it up carefully and mailed it to our former pastor, Charlie, without telling him its history.

The vision itself was one of the most prolonged in measures of time of all the visions that I have ever experienced, but the message was the slowest for me to comprehend. During the time that the vision was on the ceiling, in the first stage of the vision, it was one of the most beautiful watercolors that I had ever seen. It still had no significance to me personally. The purpose of the second stage meant nothing either, but it did lead me to study every element of the picture. I memorized the colors, tones, shape and size of each item, and the perspective that combined to make such an eye-catching design. At the exact moment that I decided that I had examined every detail, the vision vanished.

I believe that the vision appeared to me for a second time so that I would study the picture in detail. This is the way that the Lord would have for us to look at our lives and every act in great detail. He would have us to see if everything in our lives, character, commitment, and behavior are painting a picture that glorifies Him. Is there anything in our lives that is destroying the beauty of a painting that God has designed in us when he purposed our creation?

# 20

# Vision:
## MEMORIAL DAY FLOOD

A car drove out of a parking lot and clipped the rear bumper of Mil's car as she was driving down a main thoroughfare in Tulsa. Arrangements were made with the insurance company of the negligent driver to get our car repaired. It was our desire to have our son-in-law repair the car. Our daughter came from her home in Stillwater to exchange cars with us while her husband replaced the damaged part.

During the early Tuesday morning prior to the exchange, I had had a vision that lasted for only a few seconds. As I got out of bed during the night, a bright light shined down in our bedroom. It appeared to light up an area forty feet in diameter. In every direction I looked, I saw water. I felt that I was about three feet above this water as it flowed under me. I could see bubbles of various sizes on its murky surface.

This incident made a good topic for discussion between me and my close friends for the rest of that week. We thought of every spiritual interpretation as to its possible meaning. As usual, every idea that came to our minds was one hundred percent wrong.

When I woke up on Sunday morning, I got up and looked out of the window of our second-floor apartment. Below me was water, flowing water with bubbles on its murky surface. During the night, Tulsa had a storm that produced a flash flood. The first-floor apartments were flooded, but we on the upper floor had slept through the deluge. When I looked down at our car port where our car was normally parked, there was three and a half feet of water in the area. Fortunately, our car was in Stillwater being repaired. The van my daughter had brought for us to use was too tall to drive into our parking space, so I had parked it up a slope. Water never got higher on the vehicle than the hubs of its wheels. It had sustained no damage from the storm.

The messages of the vision were clear. God showed His foreknowledge of the flood by giving me a picture of it before it occurred. He took the events surrounding the accident in which Mil was involved to move the car out of an area where it would have been totaled. He had taken a very unpleasant episode and turned it into a blessing by rescuing our car from the flood.

I know there were numerous ways that the Lord could have provided me with an equal or even better blessing. I am sure He has led everyone around many problems about which they have never known just because He cares for His children. I have learned from other experiences that He will lead me through some very difficult situations to deepen my trust in Him.

When I watch films of floods, storms, and other natural disasters around the world, I always recall this vision. I know that the Lord is speaking to us through them. My thought is, *God, what are you saying*?

# 21

# Vic's Dreams:
## FASTING

When Mil and I moved to Tulsa, I met Vic. He was a member of the architectural staff of which I had become its newest employee. As we got to know each other, we discovered that we had had many similar experiences in our walk with the Lord.

We attended many Bible studies together, even though we were members of very different denominations. He was a Roman Catholic, and I was a Southern Baptist. Despite our differences, the center of both our beliefs was Jesus as our Lord and Savior.

We worked together for many years until he resigned and opened his own office. I lost track of Vic for a couple of years, and in the meantime, I retired from architectural practice.

One morning when I didn't have much to do, I thought of Vic and felt an urgency to contact him at once. As I looked up his phone number, I noticed that his office address had been changed, which disturbed me for some reason. I decided not to phone him after all.

I got my golf equipment and left our apartment to go to a practice area. I often used exercise in the outdoors as a retreat from any situation that I considered to be unpleasant. As I was getting my clubs from my car, I heard in my spirit, "You chickened out." My mind replied immediately, "Yes, Lord. There seems to be something wrong in Vic's office, and I just don't want to get involved in any more problems at the moment."

I practiced for a while, picked up balls that were scattered over the practice range, loaded my golf equipment into my car, and returned home. I had been home only a few minutes when the telephone rang. It was Vic calling.

He said, "Bill, I have had you on my mind all morning, so I just decided to call you." With that call came the knowledge that God had some plan that involved Vic and me together. Since I had chosen not to call Vic, He had inspired Vic to call me.

We continued talking about the events in our individual lives since our last visit. I had been right in thinking that he was facing some problems when I decided not to call him earlier. When he asked if we could get together, I accepted his invitation to come to his office for a chat.

None of his problems, as I recall, were unusual for a new office that was building a base of clientele. We discussed the things that we felt the Lord had been teaching us since the time when our paths had taken different directions. In many ways, the knowledge the Lord was sharing with both of us was very similar.

This was and continues to be a great source of encouragement and confirmation for each of us, as we believed that we were hearing the same message from the Lord.

Soon after our meeting, Vic called me one morning to say that he had a dream the preceding night. He wondered if I had an idea of its meaning. His dream was unlike any that I had ever experienced, and yet the message was similar to a dream I had in the past.

I interpreted it according to what my dream had meant to me and the confirmation that followed later. Vic was satisfied with my answer. This incident became a pattern over the next few weeks. About every third night, Vic had another dream and would call to ask me to tell him its meaning as I understood it.

The message of each dream he had during this brief time could be found in one of the many dreams that I had experienced over a period of several years. This experience leads me to believe that the time until Christ's return is very short, and we must work with the same haste in doing the things that are our calling.

The most interesting single event that happened during this whole episode occurred one morning during the early days of my retirement. I went to our bedroom and noticed a book I had received from Dr. Charles Stanley of the "In Touch Ministry."

It was a publication made up of many scriptural categories. I lay down on our bed and began to read at the point at which the book had opened. The theme was fasting, which interested me, so I began to read the many scriptures pertaining to that subject. Just as I was finishing reading all of the verses, the phone rang. It was Vic. After we exchanged greetings, he proceeded to tell me the purpose of his call.

"Bill, I have been praying this morning, and I believe the Lord is telling me to fast. Do you have any scriptures about fasting?"

I assured him that I did. I told him to get his pencil and start writing. I was looking at them that very instant.

# 22

# Sonja:
## TEMPTATION

Coming home on the bus after work in downtown Tulsa was an adventure. The bus ride was about seven miles long, and the walk from the bus stop was approximately four blocks. The length of the journey provided plenty of time for many of my experiences to develop.

This was a time during which the Lord was educating me in ways beyond my comprehension. At the same time, He was using me to minister to people in very surprising and life-changing ways. The Lord is the author of all these events, for I do not have the imagination to make them up on my own.

I first saw Sonja as she got off the bus. She nearly always wore a big infectious smile. She was a young black lady who walked very slow and enjoyed the scenery. I was always in a hurry to get home after the bus ride, so it was some time before we had any conversation.

I don't recall what prompted the first talk we had, but afterward we enjoyed many pleasant walks along the last part of my trip home. She shared with me that she was a new bride of a few months. Her husband worked evenings, so she seldom saw him except on weekends.

She was a newborn Christian and knew very little about the Bible. She had tried to read the King James version, but she was having a problem comprehending anything that she read.

I gave her an New Intenational Version of the Bible and suggested some books that she begin reading. Most of our walks turned into discussions about the things she had read the evening before. One of the more interesting events that the Lord has involved me in happened during one of these strolls.

I had been talking to her about various topics as they came to mind. As we were about to part, Sonja said, "Bill, I had three questions that I was going to ask you today. You answered everyone of them before I could even ask."

I was as much amazed at what the Lord had just done as she was. I had never felt that my thoughts were inspired at all as they obviously had been. Sometimes the Lord speaks to us with such a gentle voice we may not realize that He is speaking to or through us.

It was very easy to see that one day Sonja was very unhappy when she got off the bus. She was a different person from the one who had been walking home with me for the past few months. I asked her if there was anything I could do for her. She looked at me for a while and then said, "Bill, I am going to tell you something I wouldn't even tell my pastor. As you know, my husband works evenings, and I have become very lonesome. An old girl friend has been coming by and taking me to hangouts where we used to go. I have run into an old boy friend, and he wants me to go out with him again. I really want to go. I know it's wrong. The desire to go with him is tearing me up."

As I looked at her, I could tell she was very distraught. I couldn't help it, but I began to laugh at her plight. My laughter really upset her, and she demanded an explanation for my laughing at something she considered serious.

I asked, "Don't you know what has happened? Can't you see that Satan wants very much to destroy your marriage? He is the source of your desire to go out with your boy friend. Do you know where the check in your spirit is coming from? That is the Holy Spirit speaking to you. You are caught in the middle of a spiritual war. You are going to have to make a choice."

She had answered no to every one of my questions.

I continued, "Sonja, the good news is this. God could have kept this whole episode from happening to you, but

He didn't. He has allowed it to occur so that you will become a stronger person in the Lord. Go home and get on your knees and confess that you are in great need for Him to lead you through this trial. He will, and you will have certainly grown to be a bigger person through the experience."

Her big smile returned as she understood what this possibility could mean to her. That God wanted her to resist that temptation and grow from it had challenged her. I think that she left me determined to be victorious.

She shared with me during the days that followed that she was still having to fight the spirit of desire, but she was not going to quit praying.

Shortly following this time, one of us relocated to another part of Tulsa. I don't recall which of us moved. One or more years went by before I saw Sonja again. I ran into her in an office building across the street from the one in which I was employed.

She told me that she and her husband had just purchased a new home and that they were very happy. I enjoyed the thought that maybe the Lord had allowed me in some small way to be responsible for redirecting her away from a path leading to a broken marriage to the path of joy that she was sharing with me.

One evening as I was leaving work, I saw her getting into her car across the street. She saw me at about the same time and waved, then she turned to the man who was assisting her into the car and spoke to him. I turned away and was lost in thought when I felt someone tapping me on the shoulder. It was the man who I had seen with Sonja. He smile, shook hands and said, "Thanks for being a friend to my wife."

# 23

# Angels:
## FLEECE

My two younger daughters, Joyce and Jere noticed the happiness exhibited by their nephews, Charlie and Jeremy, as they rode with them. This brought about the two sisters voicing their desire to each other for children. They prayed for the Lord to give them children at the same time who would have the same affection for each other as the two cousins displayed.

A short time later, a niece of Mil's called to say that she was looking for a home for a niece and a nephew of hers. She did not want to put the two up for adoption with people that she did not know. To Joyce and Jere this was an answer to their prayer.

The children were brought to Oklahoma by their aunt. A younger brother also came at a later date to be adopted with his brother. After a while, joint proceedings for their adoption began. Joyce was residing in Chickasha and Jere in Stillwater. A court date to handle the adoption case was scheduled. Joyce engaged an attorney in Chickasha to represent both families.

The law required that advertisements concerning the impending hearing had to be run in newspapers in the last known address of the birth parents. Having a knowledge of the father's violent past, it was a complete surprise when Jim, their father, arrived to contest the adoptions.

Jim went to see Joyce's attorney in Chickasha to find his daughter, now renamed Amber. It was his intention to get her and her brother Jamy, who was with Jere in Stillwater, and take them back to his mother's home in another state.

The attorney was unable to provide him any information, so their father left for Stillwater.

Altercations occurred between Jim, a welfare worker, and a judge who would not order the welfare agency to release the location of the children to him. The welfare worker was so alarmed over the incident that she notified Joyce and Jere of Jim's intentions to take the children away.

It was at this point that the decision was made to move the children to Tulsa to be with Mil and me until the time for the hearing. At Mil's suggestion, the sisters and Mil went to see a lady, Carol, to pray for the safety of the children as she felt led.

Carol prayed that the sins of the generations would not be carried down to the youngsters. She also sensed that they should pray for the PROTECTION OF ANGELS.

The attorney in Chickasha could not be located by telephone to be apprised of the latest threat being posed by the father, so Joyce and Jere decided to drive there to seek his counsel. Meanwhile, Mil asked Jan, another of our daughters, to aid her with packing some of the children's clothes and accompanying her with the siblings to Tulsa. Jan was not aware of Carol's prayer earlier in the day. They drove to Jere's home. When she got there, Jan went to the dining room and asked the Lord for protection over the house. She was immediately aware of a very bright light shining through her closed eyes.

When she opened her eyes, she saw two angels standing on each side of a glass sliding door that opened to a patio area. They were very tall and stood with their heads bowed due to their height. They appeared to be of a white light.

She began to shout for her mother, who was in the connecting garage at that moment, to come quickly. Mil hurried into the room, but before she arrived, Jan saw the two fade slowly away. She was the only one who saw the pair and also the only one who did not know about Carol's earlier prayer for the PROTECTION OF ANGELS.

When the group arrived in Tulsa late in the evening, I was seated on a sofa reading my Bible. Jan, still very excited from her experience, told me about the visitation of the two angels. I admit that I was very skeptical of her story. I thought that maybe some light from outside of the house had reflected on the sliding glass door to the patio.

When she finished speaking, I glanced down on my open Bible, and the first word I saw was "seraphim." To me this was just a coincidence. As I thought about about her story, I decided that I would never tell about the angels unless the following happened—

I told the Lord, "If this story is true and you ever want me to mention it, have our pastor preach about angels this Sunday."

To my knowledge, he had never spoken about this subject before. I did not expect that he would on this occasion either, but I did go to the service with my ears tuned to see if he referred to the subject of angels even once.

Sunday morning came. I had told Mil about the fleece I had put before the Lord. When we entered the sanctuary, we were ready for the pastor's sermon. As the service began, we had our spiritual ears tuned. The first words out of our minister's mouth were, "And the angel of the Lord..." He went on to tell the story of Gideon and his encounters with the Lord's angel.

God called Gideon to save Israel from the hand of Midian. Gideon felt as if the Lord had abandoned Israel because the people were not seeing the wonders their fathers had told them about when the Lord brought them out of Egypt. Gideon wanted assurances from the Lord that He would be with him in all that God was asking him to do. The Lord answered both of Gideon's two fleeces, a dry fleece on the damp ground and a wet fleece on dry ground. (This story is found in Judges 6.)

God answered my FLEECE with a story about Gideon's FLEECE. When we left the church that morning, I knew beyond any doubt that two of God's protecting angels were indeed standing before Jan when she asked for God's protection on that home.

A few months following this experience, I was relating this story to a member of our church. The conversation happened between the Sunday school lesson and the morning worship service. The pastor's sermon was again about Gideon and his FLEECE. God has a way of often reminding me of past events when He has directed my thoughts with His Holy Spirit.

Note: The Judge ruled in favor of the adoption by Joyce and Jere. I believe the final disposition was determined at the time the sisters prayed for the Lord to give them children.

# 24

# Shaking:
## ECONOMY

I sensed an uneasiness in the people with whom I associated. I do not remember that I personally felt this way myself, but it seemed easy to detect something different in their attitudes. The confidence that they usually exhibited was missing.

This became even more evident one morning in my Sunday school class. Person after person witnessed that they had a very uncomfortable feeling that there was something missing in their lives or something beyond their ability to express. We left the class without any answers to our apprehensions.

Mil and I arrived early in the sanctuary before the morning worship service. I told her about the expressions of concern that I just heard. The sentiment was so general that I wondered if there was something I was missing. For the next few minutes, I pondered the possibilities for the unrest that many were feeling in their lives.

Suddenly I had a thought. I knew, in my spirit, that it was the correct answer to our perplexity. I told Mil, "I know the answer. God is preparing to shake this place."

At that moment, the pastoral staff and the choir entered. The service proceeded until it was time for the sermon. The pastor read his scripture text from Acts 4:31 NIV, "After they prayed, the place where they were meeting was shaken, and they were filled with the Holy Spirit and spoke the word of God boldly." As soon as he read that scripture, it was confirmation to my mind that there was a shaking coming. My error was that I thought it was limited to just our church.

About two months later, the economy of Tulsa fell as many of the oil companies from our location moved to other cities. The staffs of many companies that remained were reduced in numbers, and new building construction slowed markedly. The shaking had begun. Two fellow employees in our office were given notice of the termination of their jobs.

I shared with them that this transition period they were experiencing was of the Lord. I assured them that He would provide for them in some way, and that they had nothing to fear.

I said, "What is of God's, will stand. What isn't of God, will fall." When they left two weeks later, each had a job with larger salaries or more benefits than they had while being employed in our office. The shaking that I sensed years ago is continuing today, and I believe it will not cease until Christ returns. It is designed to alert us to look only to God for direction during some very discouraging times. We will only have a true peace of mind when we have our priorities in total accord with the plan God prepared for us before we were even born.

The encouraging element of this story is that God gives us clear evidence that He knows of all of our problems, such as the economy's collapse before it happens. He, therefore, knows the answer to all of our dilemmas before they arise. Take heart in every predicament and thank God for His answers.

# 25

# Jim:
# BUS FARE, RIDE HOME

Our usual group of passengers gathered at the morning bus stop. We chatted as we waited for the morning express to take us downtown to our various jobs. Sometimes we had several minutes to wait for the arrival of the bus, as this time varied from day to day.

On the morning when this particular story occurred, a young man approached our group and asked us several questions. Were we waiting on a bus? Did it go downtown? How much was the fare? And he added that he had a new job downtown, but he didn't have the fare to get there.

I doubted his story and felt that he was playing us to be rather stupid. I rode the bus back and forth to my office every day. The bus ride required exact change, so I came prepared to have that amount on me. Often I had no extra change. This was true on this date, and so I considered whether I wanted the hassle of remembering to get change again before I came home.

Then I thought of the slim possibility that he was telling the truth. I did not want to be the reason for his not being able to get to his work. I yielded to this thought and said within myself that I would give the fare as unto the Lord and forget about the matter.

Two passengers with whom I was acquainted were already on the bus when I got on. We sometimes had conversations during the bus ride and continued the discourse from the place where we got off until we had to separate to go to our individual offices.

Jim was a graduate of the Naval Academy and a top metallurgist with one of the oil-related companies in the city.

Fred was a chief accountant for another nationally known company. Their conversations were very interesting much of the time, but there were a few times that their talk disturbed me.

This occurred when one of them would relate that he was not feeling too well, and the other would suggest that they needed a touch from Oral Roberts. The statement sounded so sarcastic.

I do not want to judge anyone's personal relationship with the Lord, but I cannot keep from being concerned when I hear expressions that limit God from providing all of the blessings that He has for each of us if we but ask.

I believe most of the time this shows a lack of knowledge on the speaker's part that God can and will do more than we can even imagine. After all, He is the Creator of everything, seen and unseen, that exists.

I replaced the change I had given away in the morning necessary for my bus fare home. I had just arrived at the bus stop when Jim spotted me in the crowd. He told me he had been given a company car to keep overnight. He wanted to know if I would like a ride home.

The bus fare I had given away as unto the Lord had been returned that same day in the free transportation. I don't recall any other time during all of my stay in Tulsa that I was ever offered a ride home.

The ride home provided an opportunity to tell Jim about many of the experiences I had had with the Lord. I believe that he found them very encouraging, as most people do with whom I have shared. By the time we arrived at my home, Jim was already guessing the endings of my stories.

Occasionally after that day, I would meet Jim by chance, and he would take me somewhere were we could talk. Then he would ask me to tell him about the latest things that the Lord was doing in my life.

I have no idea of how much this incident affected Jim's life, but it was a pattern of the opportunities that God gave me to witness about His personal knowledge of our needs and His desire to provide us with answers if we would but ask in faith.

# 26

# Widow:
## Sunset, Blessing

Irene was a new tenant in our apartment complex. We became acquainted at the morning bus stop. She was a middle-aged lady who had little to say. Our first real conversion occurred after we had departed the bus and started our evening walk to our apartments.

It was a beautiful bright red and gold sunset that glowed in our face, an awe-inspiring panorama of color against a black silhouette of leafless trees and buildings. It was the Thanksgiving season, and the surroundings reminded me that we had much for which to be thankful.

I began to tell Irene that the sunset reminded me of the many blessings of the year. As we talked, I told her about some of my experiences with the Lord. Our family had seen a true miracle of healing. Our grand-daughter had received a new hip joint. It was missing from birth. We were truly thankful for all the many ways that God had answered our prayers.

Sometime later, Irene and I were walking down the same path again. I don't recall why I felt like I did, but I was in an intensely down-hearted mood. Everything in my life seemed to be pointless at that time, and my emotions expressed how low I was feeling.

When I expressed this emotion to her, she stopped, faced me, and said, "On the morning of the day that you told me about all of the things that we had to be thankful for, I had arisen very depressed. My husband passed away recently and I was very lonely.

"I told the Lord that there was no one who ever said anything encouraging to me. It was that same afternoon when your words encouraged me so much. I knew the Lord had heard me when I heard you talking. Don't ever say your life is pointless again."

Her assertion lifted my spirit. The Lord showed me again that He did have a purpose for me. One's emotions can be very deceptive and not always to be trusted.

# 27

## Oranges and Potatoes

As I listened to the conversation between two gentlemen who were discussing their beliefs, I could not help but think about the limits they were imposing on God.

I knew they were dedicated to their church, so I wondered why they harbored such thoughts as they did. I said nothing, even though I have sensed the presence of God far beyond their limitations on Him. After I retired to bed that evening, I lay awake thinking, *God, why do people make you small?*

I awoke suddenly during the night as I heard in my spirit, "You can't put oranges and potatoes in the same sack." I immediately heard it again, "You can't fill a sack with oranges and then fill it with potatoes."

I believed the statement, but I did not understand the relevance. He said, "You can't be filled with your job, your finances, your entertainment, your church traditions and be filled with my spirit at the same time. As you die to each of these portions of your life, I will fill it with my Spirit, and then you will have a BIG GOD."

*I understood that.* I thought about the illustration that the Lord had given me. There was no way that I could have come up with such a line of reasoning in my own mind.

The Lord had answered my question of the previous evening very clearly. God would fill me with His Spirit only as far as I would trust Him to be in complete charge of every portion my life. To have a big God, we must give every part of our lives over to His complete control.

One day as I was riding the bus to work, a lady I had never meet before sat down beside me. I felt the Presence of the Holy Spirit fall over me, and I knew she was about to start a conversation with me. She and her husband were going through a very difficult time financially, though she said nothing about the problem. I told her of several of the experiences that my wife and I were having with the Lord, including this story.

A few days later, she sat beside me on the bus again. This time she told me about the financial worries she and her husband had. She further stated that when I spoke of the oranges and potatoes, she recognized that the Lord was speaking to her through me. She and her husband determined to die to self-will and to be filled with the Holy Spirit by giving Him total control of their income. A short time later, our paths parted until she called me a couple of years later.

She asked me, "Do your ears ever burn? I tell the story about the oranges and potatoes over and over to most of my acquaintances."

We never really know how the things that God does in our own lives will affect and encourage others in such a far-reaching manner.

# 28

# Feed My Sheep:
## 23rd Psalm

I often woke up in the middle of the night and lay awake dwelling on various subjects. On this particular night, the theme was sheep. It centered for an extended period of time on chapter twenty-one of John.

In the fifteenth verse, Jesus asks Peter, "Simon, son of John, do you love me more than these others?"

"Yes," Peter replied. "You know I am your friend."

"Then feed my lambs," Jesus told him.

This was the object of my thoughts for a couple of hours. I could not quit thinking about sheep. I wondered why Jesus kept repeating to Peter His direction for him to minister to His sheep. I thought about all of the characteristics of sheep. I contemplated all the care that the shepherd had to give his flock. I wanted to put the subject out of my mind, so I tried to think of a new topic. I managed to direct my thoughts to the Psalm 23. I remembered an earlier vision (chapter 5) where the center of my attention was sheep.

This incident occurred early one Sunday morning. After several hours of being unable to go to sleep, I told the Lord if He did not let me sleep soon, I would be unable to go to church. I don't know when I dozed off, but I woke up fully rested.

At the beginning of the worship service, there was an announcement that the pastor would not be preaching that morning due to a previous engagement. Jerry, the youth pastor, would fill the pulpit in his place. His sermon would be his last before he left for seminary as a divinity student.

We had been friends with him since Mil and I had become members of the church. Jerry's sermon text was John

10:27, "My sheep listen to my voice, and I know them, and they follow me" (NIV).

I knew immediately as he began his sermon that the Lord had been speaking to me the night before. Jerry continued speaking about the character of sheep and all of the other meditations that had come to my mind during that sleepless period.

When his message ended, the choir sang the "23rd Psalm." That was further confirmation that God had been speaking, but I still did not understand the purpose for the incident.

After the service was over, Jerry stood at the exit door and said good-bye to many of the members. When Mil and I got to the door, there was no one else in line to speak with Jerry. I told of the connection between his sermon, the choir's anthem, and the two topics that had filled my mind for such a long period of time.

Jerry was elated to hear my story and saw this as a validation that the Lord had called him to be a preacher. I knew we both had heard and now recognized the Shepherd's voice.

# 29

## ELECTION TIME

The first and only time I have ever seen Don Nichols in person was in our drafting room in Tulsa. One of the principals of our office, also the chairman of the city Republican Party, introduced him to each one of his employees.

I probably would not have recalled his name, but he had given each of us a wooden nickel with his name on it. He did not get the support for his election from our principal, who had previously committed his support to another candidate. Nichols was almost completely unknown in the eastern part of the state.

Tulsa had two well-known candidates, one of which was highly favored to win a seat in the U.S. Senate. That evening while Mil and I were watching television together, an ad featuring Nichols appeared on the screen for a few brief seconds.

Mil said quickly, "What is he running for? He is one of the four candidates God told me He has His hand on."

I told her about my meeting him that very morning and that he was running for senator. I thought very little more about the incident until one evening a few days later when I had fallen asleep in front of the television. I awoke suddenly when another ad of Nichols was being screened. I heard in my spirit, "I have my hand on his head." That seemed greatly unlikely. The primary election was very close, and there already was a number of candidates on the Republican ticket.

Only the top two candidates would qualify for the run-off, and according to our city newspaper, Nichols would run a distant third at best. The primary elections proved the newpapaer wrong. The editorial page explained why they had been surprised when Nichols ran second and would be a participant in the next election.

They wrote that he had had a strong support group that had worked very hard in his behalf. This group would have no chance, though, of duplicating their effort against such a well-known businessman that he would be facing next. When my friend Vic and I told some of our fellow draftsmen that Nichols would be our next Senator, we were meet with incredulous smiles.

One evening while at church, I told a lady that Mil and I had heard from the Lord that a certain person was going to be elected, but I was not going to name him because I was not trying to influence anyone's vote.

The woman said, "The Lord gave me a name of a nominee also. If I tell you the correct name, will you tell me?"

I agreed to do so.

"Is it Don Nichols?"

I told her yes and then remembered that one other person I met before the election had received the same name from the Lord.

I have no idea how many people the Lord must have spoken to in similar manner. It was enough that he won the run-off, which perplexed the editorial writers, who had a difficult time analyzing his unexpected victory. They did note, however, that the Democratic nominee had been in public office too long for him to be defeated in the general election.

They did not have the slightest idea that they were playing against a stacked deck. There is no government in power that God has not placed there to serve His purpose. Read Romans chapter 13. I have no idea how long Senator Nichols will stay in the Senate, but God has used him to stand up for Christian principles while battling against worldly standards.

# 30

## DEACON'S SON

I have witnessed the healing of several people during the last few years. I know that God can and will heal, but I understand very little about when and how it will be done.

One thing that has occurred each time is that prayer is always a part of the person's recovery. In the following story, God evidenced that He not only heard our prayers but He had directed them.

A messenger came into our Sunday school assembly room with the report concerning the son of the current chariman of the board of deacons. He has been admitted to the hospital during the night in serious condition. The diagnosis was spinal meningitis.

The family had requested immediate prayer for him by the assembled gathering. As our leader began to pray, I felt the Presence of the Lord fall on me. After the opening assembly, we went to our classes.

The teacher of our group led us in prayer, and as he mentioned the ailing boy, the Presence came on me again. When our lesson concluded, I was asked to close our session. At the point, when I asked the Lord to touch the youngster with His healing power, the Lord touched me a third time.

When I joined Mil in the sanctuary afterward, I related to her all that I had experienced previously. When the pastor repeated the request for prayer again at the opening of the morning service, I whispered to Mil that I believed that the healing was all ready finished.

I suggested to her that we thank the Lord because the boy's recovery was already manifested. As the congregation prayed again for his recovery, Mil and I gave thanks for his recovery instead. The Presence of the Lord confirmed that He was listening to our petition.

At the conclusion of the morning worship, a note was passed to our minister. It said that during the service, the child's extremely high temperature had broken, and he was resting comfortably. Mil and I had thanked the Lord appropriately. He had directed us with foreknowledge through the whole affair.

Two days later, the deacon's son was discharged from the hospital—completely healed by God's loving compassion for each of us.

# 31

# Anger: I Quit

As I rode home from work, I had plenty of time to contemplate the events of the day. I did not know why, but my emotions had gone from frustration to anger to defeat. When I walked in the door of our apartment, I felt that I given my all in a certain circumstance that I thought was very important and had failed miserably. I was overwhelmed with hopelessness. I related my story of despair to Mil and I said, "I quit."

As I pondered the many experiences of my past, I began to have second thoughts about my decision. Maybe I needed to reconsider my abrupt actions. I decided to give God an opportunity to speak to me about the situation. I told Mil about my new plan.

"I am going to hold my Bible in my hands. If God shows me a verse that I don't recall, that gives me a reason why I shouldn't quit. Then I'll continue on regardless of my feelings."

I held my Bible vertically between my hands and waited patiently for it to open. (I hadn't been told not to do this by anyone at this time and the danger that could be associated with such an exercise.) The pages began to part, the book fell open, and I began to read. The verses were from 2 Corinthians 4:16, 17, 18 from *The Living Bible*:

"That is why we never give up. Though our bodies are dying, our inner strength in the Lord is growing every day. These troubles and sufferings of ours are, after all, quite small and won't last very long. Yet this time of distress will result in God's richest blessing upon us forever and ever!

"So we do not look at what we see now, the troubles all around us, but we look forward to the joys in Heaven which we have not seen. The troubles will soon be over, but the joys to come will last forever."

I was completely surprised by God's answer to my request for direction. Now when I face events that seem overwhelming, I think about this incident. It is very encouraging for me.

# 32

# Kathy, Respect:
## LISTENING

When Kathy found that I was a watercolorist, she recruited me to assist her in the teaching of her senior high-school art classes. She was the only art teacher for senior high students at Metro Christian Academy in Tulsa. I had retired from working full time in architectural work, and I was very curious as to what made young people tick.

I had heard that there was a generation gap between young people and my age, the age group of those who were born before Noah and the big Flood. This was my opportunity to discover how the young become so brilliant in their teens and then fall back to the level of only genius.

Kathy was an excellent teacher, articulate and very concerned about her students in every way. She often prayed with her classes and shared her deep faith with them. Yet everything was not wonderful in her private life.

She had become a single parent of two offspring during the time that I was there. I wanted to be an encouragement to her by lifting a part of her distress.

One evening she called me and we were discussing some phase of our teaching. Without any studied thought, I told her that I thought she was one of the best teachers I had ever seen instruct. She seemed taken aback and said, "Bill, that is the first time anyone has ever said anything like that to me. I will remember and treasure that statement as long as I live."

I awoke during the night and began to think about our conversation. What I had said was a spontaneous thought from the heart. After the reaction she had and the encouragement she received from what I said, I determined in my heart to do the same thing with others at every opportunity. At that exact instant, I heard the Lord speak to me in my spirit.

He said, "That doesn't always work." I was surprised twice by that answer. First, I didn't realize that the Lord was listening to my thoughts, and secondly, I shouldn't always speak encouraging words expecting them to be received in the manner offered.

The Lord continued, "People only listen to those they respect. Many don't listen to me. They don't pray or read my Word. Why do you think they would respect and listen to you when they don't respect me in any way?"

I got the point! That didn't mean I wouldn't try to speak words of encouragement at opportune times. I understood that I must try to earn respect first from those I am trying to help. I must not feel offended when that word is rejected.

I think it is obvious that anyone who desires to have a voice of leadership must demonstrate a character that is above reproach constantly. This character can only be built over a period of time by studying God's Word and using it as the cornerstone for your life. There is no other standard that is always a perfect model.

# 33

# Kathy:
## God Hears Prayers

How do you know when God is speaking to you? He speaks to me in many ways. Sometimes He speaks very much as is illustrated by a conversation in this story. Most of the time, I can not distinguish my thoughts from His in my mind, so I do the things that seem to be the right action at the moment.

Often when I look back at the events that follow, I can see that what seemed to be my thought was really God speaking to me. There is a third way God speaks to me, and that is silently.

During these times I hear nothing so I begin to wonder why the silence. I become much more attentive to what is going on. I examine my own actions to see if God has been speaking, but I have become too busy or indifferent to hear Him. This is a time during which I feel alone.

This is a continuation of the preceding story. I was assisting Kathy in teaching her art classes. I am sorry to say it, but I was becoming very disenchanted. There were a few very good students, and watching and listening to Kathy was a very pleasant experience. However, there were a few students that completely offset any desire of mine to continue with my efforts.

I knew there was a generation gap between my age and theirs, but to me it seemed more like two and a half gaps. A few of the students were unbelievably rude and dared you to try to teach them anything. I did not need to donate my time to that stress-filled harassing atmosphere.

I was shaving one morning at the same time considering whether or not I would go to the art classes. I made the decision to stay home.

I was plenty perturbed when I heard the Lord say, "I want you to go to school this morning."

I said in return, "I just don't want to go. I can't help those students. I can't stand some of them. They're rude and don't listen to anything. It's a complete waste of my time," I countered.

He replied, "I want you to go and help the teacher."

That was different. I got ready to face the ordeal and left immediately for the chore. When I walked into the classroom, Kathy was seated at her desk. She said, "Bill, I am so glad to see you. I have been praying that God would send you. I am very ill and I cannot afford to take the day off. Please take charge of the class."

After I had seen a few of the students that wanted my assistance, I went to her desk. I asked her if she wished for me to pray for her. She assented quickly. As I started to pray, I sensed the direction of the Lord. God was showing me that He was listening.

I returned to selectively instructing the ones I could tolerate. After a few minutes had passed, I looked up to see that Kathy was now instructing also. She smiled and said she was feeling much better.

That evening, I received a call from the school. Kathy was in the hospital with a blood disease. She had requested that I fill in for her in the meantime. I felt that I had no choice. I agreed to the sentence, if the school would provide a warden who would be in the class to suffer with me.

I endured until she came back to her class one afternoon. She was recovering in half of the doctor's expected time for healing, but she had to go home to rest until she was completely well.

She spoke to the students, saying, "I have often prayed for you by name. I came by to ask you to gather around me and do the same for me as you feel led to do so."

Two students prayed for her first, the very ones I thought would be the ones most likely to do so. The prayer of each was accompanied by God's Presence upon me. Then came a big surprise. The one student I thought would be the least likely to pray came and prayed for her. The Presence of the Lord really fell on me during the prayer he gave. He was one of the students who was on my list of "CAN'T STAND THEM." I was thoroughly humbled.   God was being attentive to someone I did not want to give the time of day. Think about this for a while, maybe a long, long while. I know I did.

# 34

## Esoteric

God has surprised me many times in my life. In fact, I can remember very few events that have not astonished me. He has told me of things He was going to do through me, but never the reason for His action or how they would be accomplished. This has kept an air of excitement and anticipation within me.

One day, while I was working at my drafting desk, my mind drifted away from the task at hand. I began to think about the numerous types of events the Lord had led me through. I know that God never makes a mistake. However, I could not keep from wondering why He would choose me for any special plan of His when there are so many better qualified people. I wondered why God had not selected someone who could articulate his or her thoughts clearly, someone who had a large audience, someone of note.

The instant I had that idea, I heard in my spirit the single word "esoteric."

I looked around to see who had uttered the word. Every one had their head bent over their work. To my knowledge, I had never heard the word before that had registered in my mind.

I wondered if it was a real word. If it was, what was its definition. My curiosity compelled me to get a dictionary and see if I could find it's definition. I hoped it was spelled like it sounded to me. I had a big surprise when I read the meaning.

Es-o-ter-ic \,es-e-ter-ik\ adj a: designed for or understood by the specially initiated alone b: of or relating to knowledge that is restricted to a small group 2 a: limited to a small circle b: PRIVATE, CONFIDENTIAL.

The meaning was clear enough. I still wonder why God picked me as I think about my qualifications. I am thankful at the same time that He did choose me for whatever His purpose.

I recognize that He is sovereign and can do anything He pleases, so I am satisfied with the manner He chose to answer my thoughts as I sat at my desk. One of the sobering thoughts that comes to mind is that God knows my every thought all of the time.

# 35

# Wanda:
## Overwhelming Fear

After Mil and I moved to Tulsa, from time to time we returned to visit the University Heights Baptist Church in Stillwater. This is the church where we were attending when God began educating us in the knowledge of His power and the plan He was preparing for us.

It was always a very interesting time for us. Pastor Charlie always unknowingly paraphrased something in his message concerning an event in our life that had occurred the preceding week in Tulsa.

As in previous times, I heard in my spirit the Lord tell me to return to Stillwater the following Sunday. I expected a typical occurance.

It was Easter Sunday. The theme of the sermon pertained to the time immediately following Christ's resurrection. The first thing Jesus always said to His fearful followers when He meet them was, "Fear not."

It was understandable that His followers would be very fearful having just witnessed the crucifixion. The Lord's message certainly made clear that He does not want us to be controlled by OVERWHELMING FEAR.

I understood the sermon, but for the first time in our attendance, there was nothing in it that connected to our lives as it had in the past. I wondered why the Lord had wanted us to go to Stillwater to hear it.

The following morning, I was working at my desk in my architectural office. I was deeply involved at some task when our secretary stopped to converse with me.

She said, "Bill, I want you to pray for me. I am going to have some tests run on me. If they are positive, I will be operated on immediately. I AM OVERWHELMED WITH FEAR."

For a few minutes it did not dawn on me what she had really said. Overwhelming fear had been the theme of the Easter message. Now I knew why the Lord had directed me to Stillwater to hear that sermon. He had reversed the usual procedure. I knew immediately my next move. It was to encourage Wanda.

I went to her work area and told her of the sermon I had just heard. I assured her that God knew all about her fear, but she really had nothing to be concerned about. God had already prepared the way for anything that was to come, and that He had confirmed it through the Stillwater episode.

She heard me and believed that what I related was true, however the fear still lingered in her mind. She called me on the office intercom two days later. "Bill, the fear just left me. Everything's going to be okay."

Wanda told me when she returned to work after the operation that the night prior to the removal of the cancer, some of her close friends had visited her in her hospital room. They thought she had been given a sedative because she had demonstrated such peace of mind while facing such a trial.

While Wanda was still recovering in the hospital, her doctor asked her to speak a word of encouragement to a couple of his patients who had a similar fear. The Lord had used Charlie's Easter sermon to give peace to Wanda and some unknown ladies in the hospital.

I wonder how often that message has been repeated to bring hope to others who are facing similar fearful experiences.

# 36

# Gift of Tongues:
## Two Reasons

Dave and I were taking our break at our architectural office in Tulsa. We were not talking about anything in particular that I recall. A question concerning the gifts of speaking in an unknown tongue and interpreting came to my mind.

I said to him, "I speak English and God certainly knows English. I wonder why He doesn't speak directly to us in the language that one understands already. There would be no need for an interpreter." We discussed the matter, but neither of us had a clue as to God's purpose.

Both of us had grown up in a denomination where we had never seen those gifts in practice. I believe God does every thing with a plan, and I do not want to miss out on anything through my ignorance. I returned to my drafting station and preceded to work on the project at hand.

Shortly afterward, the Lord interrupted my labors for a moment. He said to my spirit, "There are two reasons. The first is that there must be two witnesses to confirm my message. The second reason is I am speaking directly to a person or persons regarding something that I want to say specifically to some condition."

The answer startled me. I went to Dave's station and informed him that I knew the purpose of the two gifts. The knowledge made sense to each of us. As I walked back to my desk, my emotions were soaring. Our secretary, Wanda, was a member of a denomination where the Lord does speak in that manner at times. I wanted to impress her with my new knowledge.

I said, "I know the reason for the gifts of speaking in unknown languages and interpretations."

"What is the purpose?" Wanda asked.

I thought she was teasing me, so I did not reply.

She confronted me. "Tell me. I have experienced this gift all of my life, but I have never known the purpose."

I was satisfied that she was truly desiring to know what I had heard, so I related what I had heard from the Lord.

She thought for a little while and replied, "As I recall the incidents of this nature in my past, what you are saying is true."

She told me a story as evidence that God had her spoken to her in such a manner. She had gone through a traumatic experience in surgery only to need a second operation unrelated to the first. It was to be an operation on her larynx. Her surgeon assured her that no one had ever had this condition to heal without treatment.

Further, she would be unable to speak for about six weeks while it healed. She was very depressed.

She attended the mid-week prayer meeting in her church. She told me that she had told the Lord, "I have prayed and prayed and asked you for healing, but nothing has happened. Another operation is more than I can take. I don't believe you know where I am."

At that moment, someone began to speak in an unknown tongue and an interpretation followed. The interpreter began by saying, "I know exactly where you are...."

I don't recall the rest of Wanda's statement concerning that experience, but God had made it very clear that He was speaking to her directly concerning a very specific situation.

When Wanda returned to the surgeon for a pre-surgery examination, the larynx was perfect—operation canceled! God healed it!

# 37

# Susie:
## Another Friend

I needed some light exercise while I was recovering from a hernia operation, so I went to one of the city parks to chip golf balls. I enjoyed being outside and the peace and quiet that it afforded.

I had hit several balls at a target and was getting close to the point of picking them up with my ball retriever when I was joined by another ball retriever, a four-footed one. He was about half a dog high and a dog and a half long. He ran from ball to ball, picking them up, running with them, dropping them, and then seeking another play toy.

His owner joined us at that time to try to get control of the situation. We introduced ourselves. This is the method that God used to bring Susie and her pet, Barney, into my life. In the conversation that followed, I explained why I was in the park. The fact that I was recovering from an operation interested her.

She was a registered nurse at one of the hospitals in Tulsa. I sat down with her for a while on one of the park benches, and we conversed about many different subjects concerning our pasts. Finally the conversation turned to our relationship with the Lord.

This certainly led to our mutual desire to know more about each other. As I was about to leave, she asked if she could go with me to meet my wife, Mil. Mil was home in our apartment and not feeling well. I told her of the situation, but she still persisted in wanting to meet Mil. I took her phone number and promised her I would call her as soon as Mil felt better.

The following afternoon as I was working at my job, I thought about the chance meeting with Susie and Barney and her expressed desire to meet Mil. Her desire seemed very sincere, and yet there seemed to be something more to her request that I was not understanding. I went to see Wanda, our office receptionist secretary, to get her opinion.

I told her of the incident, my concern about calling Susie, and the role that Barney had played in our meeting each other. At that precise moment, the office phone rang. Wanda answered, she listened for a moment, became very flustered, and then opened the intercom and said, "Gary, line one please. BARNEY wants to speak with you." She hung up the phone and began to laugh. She had never witnessed such a coincidence, and furthermore she had never before even heard of anybody named Barney.

At that moment, I decided to give Susie a call. What had just happened could not have been a mere coincidence. The timing of events was too perfect.

Susie came over to dine with us a short time later. It was during this visit that she told us why she had desired to meet Mil. All of her family lived in Michigan, and she had just graduated from Oral Roberts University and had taken a job in Tulsa.

Not knowing very many people, many of her evenings were very lonely, so she had been praying to the Lord that He would give her some older friends who would be like grandparents to her. People that she could drop in on at any time to visit or go places with to fill those times when she felt lonely.

The morning she had met me in the park the Lord had told her that her prayer would be answered that day. She knew from our discussions that Mil and I were "the grandparents" God had selected for her. That was the reason for her determined quest to get acquainted with us. Our relationship with Susie was the answer to her prayers.

She visited us whenever she wished. We dined and attended a weekly prayer meeting together with some of our mutual friends. Susie was very devoted to the Lord and lived a life that expressed her deep love for Him. Together we witnessed a move of the Lord at most of these meetings.

For instance, one of her younger sisters enrolled at Oral Roberts University and began to accompany us to the prayer meetings. One evening her sister, Tammy, hobbled into our area. She had severely sprained her ankle and had come to ask for prayer. I was seated some distance from her, and as there is no distance in prayer, I decided to stay where I was. But before I could even think, I moved to sit at her feet and placed my hand on her ankle. Moments after prayer began, I felt a hand on my own ankle. I looked back to see whose hand it was that I felt, but there was no one there. I suspected this was a sign from the Lord that Tammy had received her healing.

I asked her if this was true. She nodded yes and added she had experienced a piercing pain in that ankle, and then suddenly all the pain left. We encouraged her to test the joint. She walked around the room and proclaimed the ankle was now perfectly normal. Each week God worked in different ways, and there is no way to explain the impact of this exciting time on each of our lives.

But changes in life are inevitable. Susie informed us that she was leaving Tulsa shortly. Her fiancé had graduated from a seminary in another state, and now he and some of her sisters and brothers were coming to help her pack. They would be moving her back to Michigan, where she would be getting married in the immediate future.

We were very happy for her, but we also dreaded to see her leave. She had become like a granddaughter to Mil and me.

On Monday morning her moving crew arrived. Tuesday was packing and loading day, to be concluded with the visitation of some of her friends that evening. Wednesday night would be the night when we would say good-bye. Tuesday night, however, Susie surprised us with an early visit.

Susie introduced her family, and they sat down and began some small talk. At this moment, the Presence of the

Lord fell on me. I said nothing, but I began to wonder what the Lord's plan was for the moment. Susie said they had not come to stay, but that they had come to ask me to pray for her fiancé, Dan.

Dan had injured his back while loading the moving van that morning. I knew that the healing of the back was already done. All that remained was our part, and that was prayer. I asked Dan to sit on a bench beside me and to move his back slightly as we prayed, but not so much that he would injury himself further.

Less than a minute later, Dan exclaimed that the pain in his back was gone, to which Susie expressed her great faith in the power of prayer by saying, "You've got to be kidding."

I was as surprised as she was at the quickness of the healing. Dan stood to his feet and proceeded to place the palms of his hands on the floor. Dan was healed. The group left but planned to return the following evening.

During the night, I awoke suddenly when I heard the Lord say in my spirit, "Susie."

"Susie," I repeated.

The Lord said, "How would you like to have another friend like Susie?"

The question caught me by surprise. As I began to think about it, I wasn't sure whether I wanted another friendship that close or not. When you lose a close friend, it sure does hurt, and I knew that probably we would never see her again.

I said, "Lord, right now all I know is that it really hurts, especially when I know that this friendship is over permanently." Then He hit me between the eyes verbally with a two-by-four.

He said, "Now you know how I feel when someone turns their back on me and walks away."

I knew He wasn't saying that Susie was turning her back on Mil and me. He was referring to the pain that we had just experienced. He has similar pain when one rejects His love for them.

I had never even thought about God having very deep feelings for anyone. This was a true revelation to me. When Susie and her family came to our apartment the next evening, I related the incident to her. Her response was the same as mine had been. It took time for the idea sink into our minds.

For the first time I had been given knowledge of God's deep desire, to the point of such pain, to have a Spirit-filled and personal relationship with each of His children.

We have lost track of Susie and Dan. We know that for a number of years they were missionaries in Poland. One other thing we have learned from our acquaintance with Susie. If the Lord ever asks us again, "Do you want another friend like Susie?" there will be no hesitation on our part. In a heartbeat, we'll say, "Yes, Lord. Yes, yes!"

# 38

# Wimber:
## Seminar on Healing

The Evangelistic Temple in Tulsa was filled with people from all over the country. Mil and I were members of the church that was holding a seminar featuring John Wimber.

John Wimber had been gifted by God to pray for the sick, and he traveled all over the world teaching others the principles of his gift. While Evangelistic Temple was a member church of the Pentecostal Holiness denomination, during the two-day seminar the church was filled with a congregation representing about every Christian faith.

All the members seated on the pew where Mil and I were seated belonged to the Southern Baptist convention. Wimber's lecture emphasized the scriptural basis of prayer by presenting biblical examples. He told of the manner in which the Lord had taught him to use his gift to His glory.

He said the Lord always gave him a vision of the area in a person's body for which he was to pray, and if that didn't occur, the seminar could not proceed. He further discussed his method of diagnosis of need before prayer and how to determine when the prayer had been answered. He said, "Our part is only to pray; it is God's part to do everything else."

On Saturday morning, the lecture concluded and we moved to the laboratory of experience. At the end of this service, which featured songs of praise, Wimber said that the Lord had given him a vision to pray for victims of whiplashed necks that occurred in the months of November and February.

He asked for every one who fit that description to come to the front. Fourteen people got up from their seats and came forward immediately. He then asked for every one who been wondering why the palm of their hand was burning to come to lay hands on those who had come forward for healing.

Just as quickly and without hesitation, fourteen people arose from all over the sanctuary to stand behind those who were waiting for the Lord's remedy. The exact number of those for whom prayer had been requested was the exact number as those who had been anointed with God's power to pray for them.

After the prayers and the healing had been completed, one of those who been anointed returned to his seat in our pew. We asked him about his experience. He was the choir director of a church.

He said that he had noticed the burning sensation and had just automatically responded when Wimber called them to respond. After he got to the front, he said he knew exactly for whom he was to pray. He had never before had such an experience.

Wimber again took charge of the meeting. He stated that there were many others in the audience who had come for prayer. He asked those who needed prayer to stand up, and those who were seated around them were to pray for each in the manner in which we had just been instructed.

I stood to my feet and looked for a group with which I would like to be associated. I saw a group across the room, but they did not meet the criterion of the group that I had in mind.

I started to look around for a different place to go when I heard in my spirit, "That's your group." I knew better than to look further, so I left to join them, but I was not happy with the Lord's selection. We interviewed the young lady who was the center of our attention.

She said she was afflicted with arthritis so badly that she was unable to raise her arms above her shoulders. We began to pray for her healing. I prayed but not very fervently. I feel ashamed now when I remember my thoughts at that time. Praise the Lord, that did not stop God from touching her.

As I stood behind her with my hand on her shoulder, I suddenly sensed the Presence of the Lord. I knew she had been healed at that instant, and I whispered to her for verification. She nodded yes, and then we waited until everyone stopped praying.

We did as we had been instructed to do and asked her to raise her arms above her shoulders. Her hands went high above her head. Tears began to flood the eyes of both her and her husband. I felt happy for her, but I was disappointed with my own attitude during the whole event.

I was thankful that at least I had been obedient to God's direction, even though it was counter to my preferences. Being obedient is easy when it doesn't conflict with one's desires. I better understand how Jonah felt when God selected him to go to witness to Nineveh. God had also overruled Jonah's desires in order to fulfill His plan.

# 39

# Paula and Larry:
## EARLY CHURCH

Mil and I were new members in Evangelistic Temple in Tulsa, so we knew very few of the people who were seated with us in the Sunday School class we were attending. The classroom was located on the second floor of the activities building and accessible only by stairs.

We were in the opening moments of the program when a young lady, escorted by a gentleman, came into the class. She was on crutches and obviously had some difficulty in accessing that level. She sat beside me.

A few minutes later while the teacher was in the middle of delivering his lesson, I felt a sharp pain strike me in my hip joint on the side adjacent to her. The pain was severe and did not ease up as time passed. My mind lost all focus on the lesson.

I did not believe the pain was originating from my body. My mind was flooded with supposition, and I was beginning to think that what I was feeling was an indication of her problem area. The discomfort did not leave until the meeting closed. I had noted a man who was active in the opening exercise, so I decided to speak to him about the incident.

I asked him if he knew the identity of the person and if he knew the condition that required her to use crutches. He said her name was Paula, and her affliction was rheumatoid arthritis in her hip.

I then told him about my experience that occurred during the lesson period and asked him if he had any idea what the Lord might be saying to me. He had no suggestion except that we should pray and ask the Lord for direction. I agreed and left for the morning worship service in the sanctuary.

I forgot about praying for direction immediately. Two or three days later, I woke up suddenly during the night. I heard the Lord say in my spirit, "I thought that you were going to pray about Paula."

I remembered very well what I had said, but I still did not know what I should pray, so I said, "Lord, I don't know if you want me to talk to Paula about what occurred or not, but if you do, have me run into her in the service next Sunday morning."

The church sanctuary has a semicircular configuration and many aisles that empty into the foyer. There were several hundred people in attendance, which made it very difficult to locate anyone, especially if you have forgotten again about what you had voiced to the Lord a few nights earlier.

I had to leave my seat to go to the foyer for a few moments prior to the service. As I was making my way through the crowded area, I was forced to stand still by the movement of all the people coming into the sanctuary. Unexpectedly, Paula stepped directly in front of me. Her face was inches in front of mine.

It was then that I remembered what I had told the Lord I would do if He put her in my path. Now the question that came to my mind was, "Lord, what do I do now?"

I decided to talk to her escort as they proceeded down the aisle. I trailed the couple to their seat, where I tapped her friend on the shoulder. I related all of my past experiences of the past week regarding them. I asked them if my story held any significance for them.

Her escort, Larry, assured me that it did. He had a notebook that contained many encounters of a similar nature. This was the beginning of a long friendship with Larry and Paula. He said they were organizing a weekly prayer meeting in their home. We accepted their invitation to join them.

These meetings reminded me of the proceedings in the early church as described in the book of Acts. It was always exciting to go to see the signs and wonders that the Holy Spirit had planned for each session.

The Lord directed us through some very troubling times. It was a period of growth in our faith during which we learned to let God be in complete control in every unsettling situation.

It was during this interval of our life that Mil had a vision of Paula holding a baby in her arms. Mil did not feel comfortable in telling this vision to Paula because it seemed so medically unlikely that such an event could ever occur. She confided only with me, for we did not want to impart any false hope to Paula and Larry.

Larry and Paula left Evangelistic Temple and began a branch ministry in the Vineyard denomination. Afterward, we saw them rarely. Fourteen years passed after Mil had had the vision before we learned that what had seemed impossible had became a reality. Alexandra Joie was born to Paula and Larry.

# 40

# Madeleine:
## Lord Help Me

Saturday mornings were very special days for Evangelistic Temple Church in Tulsa. These were the days of the church's outreach to many needy people who were offered both food and clothing.

As the volunteers busily worked to assemble the provisions from the storehouse, members shared their faith with those who were receiving assistance. Many of those also made requests for other needs that were recorded on forms provided by the church.

On Sunday, prior to the evening worship service, a few members came to the prayer room to pray for those requests that were made on the previous Saturday. It was the custom of those who came at this time to pray for the needs of each individual petitioner.

The director of the prayer group assigned a packet of cards to each member, who then would read and pray according to that information as he or she felt led. Other people also came during this period and prayed for the evening service or for their own individual concerns.

One night the regular director could not lead the group, and I accepted his request to substitute for him. Everything was normal until Madeleine entered the room. She was a very dedicated lady and fervent in the Lord's work.

When she went to her prayer bench, got on her knees, and began to pray intensely, I was not surprised in the least by her manner. I did not even sense the anguish in her voice, so I was not at all certain that I had heard the Lord say to me, "Go over to her."

At first I believed I had just imagined the voice in my spirit. I heard the voice again, this time a little stronger, "Go over to her."

"Lord, I don't know her," I protested.

"Go over to her." The voice was still stronger.

"Lord, I will just interrupt her."

There was no doubt in my mind that the Lord was speaking to me now. I was hunting for an acceptable excuse not to go and speak to her. It was then that I heard the voice speak authoritatively.

"Get over there." I went immediately. I knelt down beside her and placed my hand on her shoulder and said nothing. I just listened to her petition as she continued to pray unceasingly. When she finally concluded, she looked up at me and said that she had been talking that afternoon with an old friend in another city.

The friend had told her some very traumatic news. The distress was more than she could bear alone, so she asked the Lord to send someone of the group to comfort her. She added, "At the instant that I made that request, you put your hand on my shoulder."

I was amazed by the perfect timing the Lord had demonstrated. I thought of all of the urgings in my spirit that had occurred before I had obeyed them.

The Lord had known exactly to the second what He would have to do before I would respond to His instructions to go and lay my hand on Madeleine. He, therefore, certainly knew the prayer of each individual in His house of prayer.

# 41

# Pot and Potter:
## THE VOICE

There were approximately forty members of Evangelistic Temple in the chapel at a special prayer service. It was scheduled each evening for an entire week. We were all asking the Lord to bring revival.

If you looked over the tops of the pews, it appeared that no one was in attendance. We were all on our knees, and most of us were praying silently.

I, however, had a problem. I could not focus on the purpose of our gathering. I began to think about Isaiah 64:8. It reads, "And yet, O Lord, you are our Father. We are the clay and you are the Potter. We are all formed by your hand."

The significance of this verse controlled my mind for a while as I thought about it how it applied to me. Then I remembered that my praying for revival was the objective of the evening. I couldn't seem to stay with the program. My thoughts strayed back to my relationship with the Potter time after time.

My train of thought went something like this. "Father, you are the Potter and I am the clay. I see myself as a pot that has many imperfections. I give you the authority to reshape me in any way you see fit as it glorifies you. You may break me up or crush me in such a way that you are able to fill me with your Spirit. I really want to be the person that you want me to be.

These mental gymnastics lasted for several minutes. I just could not bring this exercise to an end. At this time, I realized that someone was singing. I looked over the top of the pew to try to locate the woman who was singing a hymn that I knew very well. She sang,

*"Have Thine own way, Lord!*
*Have Thine own way!*
*THOU ART THE POTTER.*
*I AM THE CLAY.*
*Mould me and make me*
*After Thy will,*
*While I am waiting,*
*Yielding and still."*

Slowly I realized that it was the lady who was on her knees next to me who was singing very softly. I knew who she was, but I had never been introduced to her. Then my thoughts exploded. God had heard every commitment I had made. He had been reading my mail.

When the service ended, I left immediately. As Mil and I drove home, I related the incident to her. Now I had a new problem, and my curiosity was killing me. What prompted that lady to sing that song at that time? I had to know.

I determined to speak to her the following evening if she came to the meeting. When I saw her the next night, I introduced myself and then related to her my experience of the preceding service.

She began to laugh as she replied, "As I rode home with my husband, I told him what I had heard the Lord say to me as I was praying. He said for me to sing, `Have Thine Own Way.' I replied that I couldn't sing. He repeated the instruction.

"I told him that I would disturb every one in the service. He repeated the same thing to every excuse I gave Him until I yielded. I said, `Okay Lord, but I am only going to sing very low.' The Lord was silent after that."

Now we knew the rest of the story. God's hand was in the episode from its earliest conception. Don't ever, ever make a commitment to the Lord if you're not going to honor it. It is better to stay silent than to make a vow to Him, because God hears every word you say!

# 42

# Meriam:
## Divorce, Reconciliation

I don't recall the first time I felt the Presence of the Lord fall on me when I sat down in a dentist's chair or got on the examination table of a physician, but it has happened often. Each time was definitely a personal assurance that the Lord was with me through all the procedure that followed.

When this occurred again as I sat in the dental hygienist's chair, I assumed that this presence had the same significance as I had experienced before in similar situations. This was my first appointment with Meriam, so we introduced ourselves and made some small talk.

I don't remember what I said, but it affected her so emotionally that tears began to flow from her eyes. She informed me that she was preparing to file for divorce that morning. I asked her if I could pray for her, and she responded by taking my hand.

Fortunately, I have very little work in my mouth for hygienists to do, so we spent most of my appointment time talking. I shared some of my experiences under the Lord's guidance and then listened to her as she talked about the things that had brought her to the point of seeking a divorce. She told me there had been no violence by her husband, but they had just not been able to build a solid relationship together. Presently, they had been separated for about six months.

All of her close friends had encouraged her to divorce him, except for her brother, who had advised her to wait. The only thing that came to my mind at that moment was to offer to talk to her and her husband if they wished. She said she would contact him at once and try to see if they could come over to my apartment either that night or the following one. I was glad to help out if I could, but I was surprised by her haste to reconcile the situation.

That afternoon I was seated in our apartment when suddenly I felt the Presence of the Lord fall on me. Immediately the phone rang. I told Mil that I knew who was making the call. That is always easy to do when the Lord is in complete control. Meriam was calling me to confirm a time for her visit. Her husband had agreed to accompany her, which was not much of a surprise.

Most of our conversation centered around the stories that I related concerning the Lord's revelations to me. The husband began to recall some events in his past that at the time he thought were coincidences. Now he began to see them in a different light. I assured him that we are all different and unique in the Lord's sight. God had a special plan for his life alone. By the time he and Meriam left that evening, they were holding hands. I assumed that reconciliation was accomplished. I was mistaken.

When I went to her office for my next six-month appointment, she told me they were still separated but that they were dating occasionally. I was very disappointed to hear that because I like unpleasant events to conclude quickly. There was still hope, so Meriam promised to tell me if and as soon as reconciliation transpired.

A few months later, I made a big mistake. I complained to the Lord that I never got to know how the events He had involved me in worked out. A tooth broke off, so I had to make a dental appointment for a repair job. This is not the way I would have chosen to satisfy my curiosity.

When I arrived for my appointment, my dentist had an emergency in his office and could not see me right away. Meriam had had a cancellation, so she had no work to do at the moment. As I waited to see the dentist, we had plenty of time to discuss the events of the past few months. I was happy to hear that she and her husband were back together again.

As she smiled, she said she never realized how good marriage could be. Her friends said the man she was living with now was a different person from the one she had first married. The Lord certainly had His plan for the restoration of her marriage before I first sat down in her chair at the dentist's office.

Before I left her office, she added one more footnote to the story. She said on the morning of my first appointment as I prayed for her, she could not see me sitting in her chair. She saw only a light emanating from that area. She made up her mind that she was going to follow any advice I suggested to her. God works in ways far beyond my imagination to reveal His compassion and power.

# 11, 24, 42:
## Governments

I have no idea how or when I first became aware of these numbers becoming a part of my life. When it became apparent by their repetition that they possibly had some purpose, no plan was evident to me. I began to notice that when I glanced at my digital watch, alarm clock, speedometer, gas pump, sales slips, etc., the last two or more digits would be one or more of these numbers. I often awoke in the night and would notice one of these numbers on the face of our alarm clock. I told my friend, Vic. This same occurrence was beginning to happen to him as well. We decided that its purpose was possibly to give us an awareness of His presence every place we went.

The very subtleties of the whole episode makes it very hard to describe. The numbers never occurred when we looked for them. They would emerge completely unexpected and oftentimes would happen several times consecutively. I tried to calculate the chances of their repeating in an unbroken chain. The chances were incalculable. It wasn't until years later that I received my answer to this mystery of the numbers.

I went to Miami, Oklahoma, to visit Aunt Flora and Uncle Clarence. Uncle Clarence had collected a large library of books pertinent to biblical topics. One of the books dealt with biblical numerology. Of course, the numbers that had been the subject of my thoughts for such a long period of time were the first to get my attention.

These numbers and only these numbers deal with government. The numbers 11, 22, 33, etc., related to man's government as the 11 apostles. The number 24 related to God's government as the 24 elders sitting on their thrones. The final number 42 represents a government of man that is a counterfeit of God's government. It has at its heart the spirit of anti-Christ.

Our national polls reflect the degree to which our citizens approve the values of this country's 42nd administration. They are approving the values of man's government. Our government has become a counterfeit of the nation that was dedicated to God by its founding fathers. Our Supreme court has ruled that this nation and its schools are no longer under God. The situation is perilous.

Separation of church and state is not possible if the leaders of our nation are to legislate with His wisdom. Without God, there will be only confusion of mind and dilemmas beyond solution. The Holy Spirit will not lead where He is not welcome. Only if those who are called by His name will get on their knees and repent of their wicked ways will He heal our land.

# 44

## Aunt Flora:
### CANCER

Aunt Flora had been occupied with the care of Uncle Clarence for many months. He was bedfast, the victim of a stroke. She was determined to see that he received the best of care. She kept a practical nurse in the home at all times to assist him.

I didn't know she had another problem until I was informed that she was scheduled for an operation for cancer in the Joplin Regional Hospital. Mil and I left for Joplin immediately. After the operation she assured me that the surgery had been successful.

I went to visit her each day and thanked the Lord that the cancer had been removed. With each time of supplication, I sensed the the Presence of the Lord. She had not allowed the surgeon to tell me the true facts regarding her condition.

He had been unable to remove any of the cancer because it had spread too far. She refused to consider chemotherapy. It may have been better that I did not know her true condition when I was praying for her, as my faith might have been severely tested.

When Uncle Clarence passed away a short time later, Aunt Flora was in good health. I managed to visit her from time to time and sometimes took her to her physician for a checkup. It was during one of these visits that she admitted to me the real condition of her health and the reason she had not wanted anybody to know the truth. She had not wanted Uncle Clarence to learn of her illness. She knew that his days would be filled with concern for her, making their joyful relationship impossible.

Her physician was monitoring her condition for signs of the expected deterioration of her health. When the change did not occur, he decided to do a series of tests. He was amazed at the results. He found no trace of the malignancy. The Lord had healed her completely.

# 45

## Let Me Know:
## Jig Saw Puzzle

I am a very curious person. Anything I get involved in, I want to see the final result. I ask myself if there is anything I could improve if I encounter a similar incident again.

The Lord has allowed me to be His instrument in ministering to the needs of others in literally hundreds of incidents since 1975. The power that God displayed in many of these matters was always awesome as well as surprising in its development.

It was a time of education for me also as well as for many new acquaintances as God was revealing Himself in new and varied ways. The downside of this education was that I had an insatiable curiosity to know God's plan in every new instance. I tried to learn from all of the various aspects of each happening.

I know where very few of the people with whom I shared these happenings are living at this time, much less if the experience continues to be an influence on their lives. When most of these people are no longer a part of our lives, there seems to be something missing or a lack of finality to complete each story.

The Lord gave me an answer to this quandary in a way that I could never have imagined. I told Mil one day that I felt like a single piece of a thousand-piece jigsaw puzzle. I knew my exact shape. I knew my pattern of colors. I knew exactly nothing about the big picture of which I was a tiny part. I had absolutely no clue as to the design of the painting.

For three days, I continued to talk to Mil about how I felt like an insignificant part of the big puzzle. On the third day, Mil received a letter from her sister, Gay. She and her husband, Bud, live at the mid-elevation level of the Sierra Nevada Mountains.

Gay wrote that they had been snowbound for about two weeks after Christmas and that they were suffering from cabin fever. Fortunately, they had received a thousand-piece jigsaw puzzle as a gift, which had kept them occupied. Bud had finished the puzzle.

The picture was beautiful, but THERE WAS ONE PIECE MISSING. They couldn't find it. They knew what it looked like, for they could see all of the colors that surrounded the hole, and the shape of the missing piece was evident.

God spoke to me clearly through that letter. He utilized the same article with which I had identified myself, one piece of a thousand-piece jigsaw puzzle. I am a part of God's beautiful big picture. I have His assurance that I am in His plan, even though I may never get to see His Big Picture while I'm here on the earth.

# 46

# Stroke:
## THIS IS THE DAY

God knows the valleys that lie ahead of us. Sometimes when we find ourselves in that location, we find that God has already prepared a path for us. This was the case for me after my wife, Mil, had her stroke.

Often I would awake in the night and meditate about the many things we have experienced together since the summer of 1975. Such a time of reflection occurred just a few days before Mil's stroke. My thoughts were centered around "faith" during this night when the verse, "This is the day that the Lord has made, we will rejoice and be glad in it," interrupted my train of thought.

I pushed that thought away, for it did not fit into "faith" in any way that I knew. This same pattern happened again and again for an hour or more. I finally gave up trying to think about "faith" and concentrated on the verse instead. I had very little insight concerning the complete meaning of the scripture as I finally drifted off to sleep.

Our radio alarm clock that was tuned to a Christian station sounded its wake-up call. The song that the station had selected to air at that moment was:

"This is the day,
    This is the day,
This is the day that the Lord has made,
    That the Lord has made.
We will rejoice,
We will rejoice and be glad in it."

I knew the Lord had been speaking to me and directing my mind because of several past experiences, but I had not grasped the significance yet.

A short time later, I went to Miami, Oklahoma, for a weekend visit with Aunt Flora. Her age had made it to difficult for her to continue to attend her church regularly, so we listened to the ministers on TV that she enjoyed.

When one of them, Adrian Rogers, began his sermon about, "This is the day that the Lord has made," he had my undivided attention. He compared yesterday, today, and tomorrow. He said that yesterday was gone, and I could not change it. All I could do was learn from my past. Many of the worries concerning tomorrow will never happen except in my imagination.

Today, at this very moment, is the only time I have any control over. The choice that I make now is the only one that is important. Our futures, good or bad, are always determined in this manner.

We will rejoice and be glad in this day if we allow God to lead us in making a decision that glorifies Him, or we may live to deeply regret our determination if we choose to ignore Him. We cannot serve two masters. We cannot serve God and serve the devil. We will grow to love one and hate the other.

When I came home from work a few days later, I found Mil sitting in a chair. It was obvious at a glance that something was badly wrong with her. I called 911 and then our physician immediately. After the ambulance paramedics had arrived, I called the family about the emergency and then proceeded to the hospital.

The family had gathered before we could see Mil and the doctor. He gave us his prognosis and asked us if we would like for him to lead us in prayer. Of course we did, and when he began, the Presence of the Lord fell on me. I knew by that that the Lord would answer the doctor's prayer in His timing in a way that would glorify Him.

Over the course of the next few months, Mil and I became very well acquainted with some of the nurses in the rehabilitation center. One particular nurse was a very strong and encouraging Christian. I asked her what would be the evidence of Mil's recovery. She said Mil would move the toe of her paralyzed leg.

One way I knew the Lord was with us during this trying time was that often His Presence would touch me. Then moments later some friend or family member would appear. One afternoon, when I was sitting with Mil as she sat barefooted in a wheelchair, I felt this Presence. I watched the door to see who was coming, but no one came. I glanced at her foot and her toe moved. Her healing had begun.

Mil was dismissed from the center and returned to our apartment. Adapting to a new and confining lifestyle was very difficult and at times very discouraging. It was at this time that God chose to encourage me.

I had a dream in which Mil walked by me not paralyzed in any way. Even while I was dreaming, I knew this was a dream. As I had that thought, I heard the Lord say in my spirit immediately, "This is NOT a dream."

Mil has not been totally healed yet, however three other people at various times have had similar dreams of seeing her completely whole. I believe that her healing will come in God's good timing.

# 47

## CROSSING THE BAR

The uniqueness of individuals at the time of death, those who leave and those who remain, is apparent to me as I recall the final days of my parents and Aunt Flora and Uncle Clarence. God made His presence known in every instance in a way to bring peace of mind to those who knew the departed best.

MY FATHER: My dad was in the hospital for what was to be the final week of this life. In some cases, due to the very different personalities of people, it is hard to determine their relationship with the Lord. It is a time also when those most close to them desire deeply to have the assurance that they know Christ as their Lord and Savior. This was my concern during this period.

My parents' pastor came to our room during the week to visit our family. As he was about to leave, he asked my mother if there was anything he could do for her. Of course, she asked for prayer.

As he prayed, he made a statement to the effect, "Lord, we thank you for the assurance that all is well in our relationship with you."

With that statement of fact, the Presence of the Lord fell on me. I had my own personal assurance that Dad's relationship with God was guaranteed. A day or two later, the pastor returned and prayed again at the family's request.

He said, "Lord, we thank you that you have already prepared a home of many mansions for us."

Again as before, the Presence of the Lord fell on me. He had doubly assured me that we will meet again someday.

UNCLE CLARENCE: I know of no person on this earth that I have known who showed more commitment to his

Lord than this man. He was a man of integrity who had great joy in doing the things that God laid on his heart. His good humor blessed everyone, and as far as I can recall, he never spoke a hurtful word about anyone. In like manner, I have never met anyone who knew him who ever said one offensive word about Uncle Clarence, regardless of their convictions.

About ten days before Christmas of 1992, the Lord told me in my spirit that something was going to happen on that day. I had decided to spend that day in Miami visiting Uncle Clarence and Aunt Flora. Uncle Clarence had spent many months bedridden as the result of a stroke and was at his home under the care of a practical nurse, Linda.

When I arrived in their home the day before Christmas, he had slipped into a coma. Of course I immediately wondered if his passing was to be the event that the Lord had spoken about that was to occur on the following day. His condition remained unchanged until very late on Christmas day.

As I was visiting with Linda beside Uncle Clarence's bed, Linda saw some change in his condition. She told me to summon Aunt Flora, who had stepped out of the room, at once. We were standing about his bed for only a very short time as Linda checked his pulse.

Suddenly, I felt the Presence of the Lord in an unusual way. The power of His Spirit originated at my feet and sweep upward over my head with a very strong surge. Uncle Clarence's spirit left his mortal body at that instant.

MOTHER: Aunt Flora cared for Mom several years after Dad died. I was caring for Mil, who had suffered a stroke, and was unable to tend to the needs of both Mil and Mom by myself. It finally came to a point where Aunt Flora could not care for Mom either, so she was moved to a rest home in Stillwater. My moment of rest from caring for Mil was my hobby, painting watercolors.

I had just finished my latest work. It was the first painting of a sunset that I had ever attempted. As I was critiquing my product, my daughter, Judi, called. The hospital notified her that we should come to the hospital immediately. When we arrived, Mom had slipped into a coma. As we sat down beside her bed, the Presence of Lord fell on me and remained for a few minutes until the sun set for Mom for the final time.

AUNT FLORA: Aunt Flora had a stroke and was confined to her bed in her home in Miami. I was unable to spend much time with her because I had to care for Mil. Aunt Flora had a very close friend, Dolly, who offered to help. She supervised the needs and the around-the-clock nursing care that was required.

Dolly spent some time every day with Aunt Flora making sure that the staff of five were providing every service. One of the staff members was Donna. She had been working for Aunt Flora for many months prior to her illness. Donna's love for my aunt was very evident in both word and action.

Aunt Flora's health began to slip so drastically that we had to take her to the hospital for special treatment. The home staff went with her.

One morning, Dolly had a dream, in which she was entering Aunt Flora's room and saw my aunt getting out of her bed. Dolly said, "Where are you going?"

Aunt Flora replied, "Home."

"You can't go home with all of those tubes connected to you."

Aunt Flora asked her, "Who is going to stop me?"

Dolly awoke at that point, quickly dressed, and went to the hospital. She met Donna there, who informed her that Aunt Flora had just left for her heavenly home. Donna's experience during these last moments had been just as profound. She had told Aunt Flora that she loved her.

Aunt Flora had responded with the same sentiment. Then Donna asked if she could do anything for her. Aunt Flora replied, "You have done all for me that you can do." With that statement, she closed her eyes and went home to be with the Lord and Uncle Clarence.

During the night before her funeral, I awoke and began to think about 1 Corinthians 13:4-7, which exemplified her attitude about life.

"*Love is very patient and kind, never jealous or envious, never boastful or proud, never haughty or selfish or rude. Love does not demand its own way. It is not irritable or touchy. It does not hold grudges and will hardly even notice when others do it wrong. It is never glad about injustice, but rejoices whenever truth wins out. If you love someone you will be loyal to him no matter what the cost. You will always believe in him, always expect the best of him, always stand your ground in defending him.*"

The service was concluded at the cemetery. The pastor's text was the same as the scripture I had meditated about during the night. God gave a sense of closure for all of us who were so devoted to her.

# 48

# Dream:
## New Beginnings

I looked into the mirror as I began to shave, but the face I saw was not mine at my present age. I recognized the image before me; however, it was my face at about eighteen years of age.

This was the beginning of a dream that occurred about the same time as the vision of the Memorial Day flood. I was greatly surprised at my youthfulness, and I summoned Mil to come quickly. I believed if she did not come at once, she would not get to see my face when I was about forty years younger.

Sure enough, as she walked into the room, my countenance became that of my actual age. I asked the Lord for the meaning of the event. He said in my spirit, "A NEW BEGINNING."

About two weeks later, Mil and I returned to our former church home in Stillwater. The pastor who had been such a part of our first experiences during those early days was still there. He and his wife had just become parents of a new daughter two days before our return.

He didn't pass around pictures of the new arrival as he threatened to do, but he did play a tape recording of the first cry after her delivery. He then announced her name. It was April, which he explained meant, "A NEW BEGINNING."

I know that this was a confirmation of my dream. Whether my dream was a herald of the birth, or of a new beginning for Mil and me, I don't know. It has not been unusual for the Lord to do some exercise in our lives long after He has initially revealed His assurance of its happening.

I am still captivated with the likeness of myself at such a young age. As I recall the Lord's promise of a new beginning, I wonder if I can grasp any of the true meaning portrayed in that night vision.

# 49

# Shaffer:
## ENOCH

The bus ride home from the architectural office in the late afternoon usually took from forty-five minutes to an hour. Sometimes I spent this time visiting with a fellow passenger and other times meditating about various subjects.

I recall one such evening when the subject that came to mind was Enoch. I remembered that he had never died, but was taken up by God. My curiosity continued to deepen as I wondered why that happened.

During Mil's and my evening meal, I thought about Enoch again. I told Mil about my interest, and we decided to get a concordance and study about the character of the man who had so moved God to take him.

Geneses 5:22 says that after Enoch became the father of Methuselah, Enoch walked with God 300 years. The twenty-forth verse stated that Enoch walked with God; then he was no more, because God took him away.

From this statement, we gathered that the relationship between God and Enoch was on a basis of Enoch's constant awareness of his being in the presence of God over a long period of time. This was a very small bit of information, but it said a lot to us. Enoch's friendship with God represents the ultimate of relationships that is available for all of God's children.

The following night, we attended our church service to hear a visiting pastor. The minister was Dan Shaffer, the pastor of Cross Roads Cathedral in Oklahoma City. He began his sermon with, "I am going to talk about a person in the Bible of which there is very little known. But in God's eyes, he was very special, so much so that he never died. His name was ENOCH."

He continued his message by pointing out the verses that Mil and I had studied the preceding evening. I have not been given the gift to expound on Enoch's life as the pastor did, but I do know that God had been in the midst of my thoughts during that bus ride the night before.

This story was very important to Mil and me. It was typical of many such experiences. We knew that God was preparing us for some future plan. He was speaking in a still quiet voice. We were learning to listen.

# 50

## Sharon:
## Forgiveness

Dozens of passengers congregated at the bus stop to catch their bus after work. To this day I wonder why Sharon singled me out from the crowd each evening to talk as we waited for our bus. She was in her late teens and employed in the downtown area of Tulsa.

The first day I met her, she came directly to me and proceeded to introduce herself. I was a little taken aback by her bold manner, but I learned to listen to her for a few minutes each day. She usually told me about her experiences with her friends on the night before.

I wanted to be polite, so I tried to show some attention to her chatter. Slowly, I began to interject my interests into our daily chat. I quizzed her about the goals she had for her future and how she might accomplish them. Our friendship deepened through time.

Three different events happened that I remember well as I recall our association. I wondered why she continued to talk with me each evening. One day, she volunteered the answer. She said, "Bill, do you know why I like to talk to you? It's because you never put me down."

The second event occurred when she came to the bus stop in an obviously distressed state of mind. She said nothing which was completely out of character for her. She just stood beside me silently with tearful eyes.

I remained quite also until my bus arrived. "I don't know why you feel as you do," I said, "but I want you know that I care." Nothing more was ever said about her difficulty on that day. It wasn't necessary, because afterward, she returned to be the happy spirit she had been before.

The last incident was probably the most important for her maturity as an adult. She approached me in an agitated state that even showed through the mask of makeup she wore. It was obvious that she was deeply disturbed about something.

She stared at me and said, "Do you think that one can get so mad that they could kill?"

"No doubt about that," I replied, "But you couldn't. You would cool off too quickly and you are not stupid."

She relaxed a little and continued talking about the event that had infuriated her so much. Her boss had done something that brought about her intense emotion. She never confided with me as to the exact reason for the conflict.

"my supervisor and my mother are very good friends," she said. "When I tell my mother what happened, she is going to take my supervisor's side, which will only lead to a big argument. I just can't face tonight. I don't even want to go home."

I questioned her, "Does your supervisor know that you are so offended by her action?"

"No," she replied.

"Are you are the only one who is angry?" I asked.

"That's right," she said.

I said, "It seems to me that you are wasting your time. The only one who is irritated is you. It's not fair that you are the only one getting hurt. Forgive your boss of whatever happened and forget it. That way, no one will be angry, and you won't have a bad evening to endure."

My bus began loading at that time. I gave her one last word of advice. "Don't say a word to your mother about this when you get home. We'll talk about this subject some more tomorrow. Promise?"

When I saw Sharon coming toward the bus stop the following afternoon, she was wearing a big smile. She stopped and faced me.

"I learned a great lesson today that I will never forget. When I got to my desk this morning, there was a note lying on it that was addressed to me. It said, `FORGIVE ME,' and was signed by my supervisor. I'm so happy that I listened to you."

One evening when Sharon didn't show up, I noticed a man she had greeted from time to time. We sat together on a bus, and through our conversation, I was able to find out a little more about her past. I told him about her desire to talk so much to me and the development of our relationship.

He said it didn't surprise him in the least. He went on to say how her stepfather was always telling her that she would never amount to anything. "You were encouraging her, and that was the thing that she needed to hear. Naturally, she wanted to talk to you."

I never saw Sharon again. I believe on the day that I first met her the Lord led Sharon to me through that crowd of people. We both learned much through the relationship that developed between us.

# 51

# My Desire:
## SCHULLER

I have learned by experience that God knows my every thought, yet I have never ceased to be surprised when He confirms it at a latter time. This has occurred to me many times, but never with such assurance of a promise as in this account.

Mil and I were spending our weekends with my parents as part of the care that was required for their needs. We had retired for the night, and as often happened, I lay awake.

This particular night my thoughts turned to one subject. It was, *What would be my number one desire if I could have anything that I wanted*? It didn't take very long to come to the conclusion. It would be to hear the Lord say, "Well done, good and faithful servant," when I see Him face-to-face.

That would be an eternal blessing for me. It would indicate that my life's commitment and service to the Lord was truly in His will. I continued to meditate on the thought until I drifted off to sleep.

When I awoke the following Sunday morning, I turned on the television beside our bed. Pastor Robert Schuller's *Hour of Power* came on the screen. The first words I heard from him were, "And when you cross over the river Jordan, how would you like to hear the Lord say, 'WELL DONE, GOOD AND FAITHFUL, SERVANT'?"

There is no doubt that the Holy Spirit prompted the question concerning my number one desire in my mind on the prior evening. After I answered the question, God confirmed through Dr. Schuller that He had heard my conclusion. Sometimes when it seems that life is filled with difficulties, I recall this overwhelming evidence, and I get the reassurance that their is no problem too big for His answer.

# 52

# Heart Attacks:
## CONTINUING STORIES

I am an expert in what a heart attack feels like both real and fake. Six times I have experienced this pain, and it hurts very much in both situations. Not being able to distinguish the difference between the two conditions is the subject in the final chapters of this story.

The first time this happened to me, I was showing a watercolor painting I had just completed to a friend. We were both employees in the architectural office of the OSU physical plant department. Suddenly, I felt that I had been kicked in the chest.

The pain was excruciating, and I could hardly breath. This event happened only a few months after the Lord had begun to do some daily "coincidences" in my life. So when this pain hit me, I immediately believed it was something of this nature. I didn't understand the meaning for the discomfort at the time.

I was at my desk the following morning, when I heard someone say that my friend had gone to the hospital during the night. Tests were being run on him, for they suspected that he had suffered a heart attack. This condition was confirmed as a fact, and he remained in the hospital to begin his recovery for a while.

I visited him during this stage of his recovery and shared with him the happenings that were occurring in my life at the time. Because of the new revelation the Lord was showing me that I had never seen before, I assured him that I was convinced there would be no permanent damage to his health.

About three days later his physician released him. He said that there had been absolutely no damage to his heart.

I was on my way home from work when the second "attack" occurred. I was residing in Tulsa at the time and was having a pleasant conversation with Sonja, a new friend. We were riding the evening bus to our apartments and had just negotiated a sharp corner when it seemed as though someone punched me in the chest with an unseen fist. I tried not to show my discomfort, but I failed. Sonja asked me what was wrong when she noticed my obvious discomfort.

I told her that it was only a fake heart attack, and I related my earlier experience to her. This was the opening for sharing with her some of the many past events in which the Lord had led me.

The following evening, I was seated with a young man that I knew slightly. We had not conversed about things of the Spirit, but he had made a remark that though he had been raised in a Christian home, he was of the opinion that his parents' beliefs were mostly emotional.

At the exact locale as the previous evening's "attack," as our bus turned the sharp corner, I had another attack of severe pain. Try as I might, I could not cover it up. The young man inquired as to the reason for my facial expression.

I explained to him that I had suffered a fake heart attack. He looked at me questioningly and asked if I could explain what I meant by fake heart attack, for this was new to him. I told him about the past episodes when this had occurred. I explained that Satan had tried to kill me, but stupidly he had picked the same point on the route to try it two nights in succession.

He was deeply interested, especially when we began to discuss the fulfillment of prophecy in the latter days. When we parted, he said he was going to have to reconsider all of his past beliefs.

On the following Sunday morning as Mil and I were leaving for church, I heard an automobile horn honking behind us. It was the young man I had talked to on the bus, and he was picking up his girl friend who lived in our complex. They were very neatly dressed. I know that he wanted me to see they were heading for church.

Because of these past events, when I was hit for the fourth time with a stunning blow to the chest, I tried to ignore the suffering. Mil and I had moved to Stillwater, and the attack occurred while I was driving back to Tulsa on some unfinished business. A few minutes later, the pain subsided.

When I arrived in Tulsa, I had lunch with my friend, Vic. After our meal, we were returning to his office, and I was climbing a stair when severe pain shot through my chest. I sat down and refused to believe that it was anything more than Satan's assault on me.

That same day, I was seated in the living room of my son-in-law, Ron, and my daughter's home. This time I managed to cover up the excruciating feeling that struck me. Never did I believe that my heart was failing. The next morning, Joyce, her youngsters, and I went to her church.

A visiting minister delivered the sermon that morning. He was supposed to be at Evangelistic Temple for a week, but the Lord was working through him in another church in Ft. Worth at that same time. The Lord told him to come to Tulsa for that one service and then return to the church in Texas.

He was not sure of his purpose for coming, if it was for the sake of many or only one individual. The particular gifts that the Lord had given him were the message of knowledge and of healing. By the time the service started, there were several hundred worshipers in attendance. Most of them had come to have the evangelist pray for them personally as he used the gifts the Lord had given him. I was one of those.

The service went very slowly as he ministered to each person individually. When the time approached twelve noon, the minister said that anyone who wished to leave could do so, but very few did.

I had promised Mil and Jan, who was taking care of Mil's needs, that I would try to return to Stillwater by four o'clock that afternoon. If I had lunch and returned by that hour, I calculated that I would have to leave the service by 1:00 p.m. sharp.

That was the deadline I gave the Lord if He wanted me to meet with the minister. At 12:45 p.m. no one was leaving the sanctuary. At that moment the minister announced that every one desiring to have prayer should line up in the foyer that wrapped around the semicircular seating area.

Joyce and I were slow getting into line, and we were almost at the end. I knew there was no way possible I would see the minister before one o'clock. I was pleasantly surprised when he decided to begin at our end of the line.

I had a digital watch I was viewing closely. At twenty seconds to one, he was praying for the person beside me. As he placed his hand on my head, my watch read 1:00:00. Perfect timing again.

Then this man, whom I had never seen before or spoken to, said to me, "The Lord says that He is giving you a new heart. YOU WILL NEVER HAVE ANOTHER HEART ATTACK. God bless you from your feet to the top of your head."

A short time later, I was examined for a possible heart problem and was given an EKG. When the test was over, the specialist assured me that my heart was perfect. By faith, I already knew that.

# 53

# Oppression:
## SPIRITUAL WARFARE

I do not recall the first time I felt the Presence of the Lord because it has developed and increased in strength over the years. However, I do recall the time and location I felt the spirit of oppression at a specific street corner in Stillwater.

The feeling was like having a steel band around my head just above my eyes. The band seemed to be slowly tightening and gave me a sensation that I was being oppressed. Afterward, the spirit of oppression always came on me whenever I passed that street corner. It made no difference whether or not I was thinking about the aberration.

I began to understand the purpose for this sensation during my stay in Tulsa. Several times when I came into the presence of strangers, I had this spirit of oppression fall on me. It was not that the individuals were evil in any sense of the word. They were simply being spiritually oppressed in some manner.

When I worked up the courage to ask them if this was true, they always replied in the affirmative. Although I didn't know their difficulty, I always assured them that the Lord knew of the problem and had an answer for them. This affirmation always lifted their spirits, and usually they confided in me the nature of their predicament. Later on the Lord expanded the meaning of this spirit. Ron and Joyce invited Mil and me to have dinner with them at a restaurant in Tulsa. The meal was served in courses, which required that we spend most of the evening enjoying the food. I began to sense this unpleasant presence around my head while we were dining.

It was too strong for me to simply ignore and continued to come and go as the evening progressed. The tightening became more intolerable with each passing moment. I told Ron and explained that I felt that I was in the center of SPIRITUAL WARFARE going on around me.

I could not see anything in the room that suggested that there was anything visually amiss. The unpleasantness never left me until we departed the premises.

The following morning Mil and I went to church at Evangelistic Temple. The service progressed to the point where Pastor Dan Beller read the text for his message. It was from Ephesians 6:11-17,

*"Put on all of God's armor so that you will be able to stand safe against all strategies and tricks of Satan. For we are not fighting against people made of flesh and blood, but against persons without bodies—the evil rulers of the unseen world, those mighty satanic beings and great evil princes of darkness who rule this world; and against huge numbers of wicked spirits in the spirit world.*

*So use every piece of God's armor to resist the enemy whenever he attacks, and when it is all over, you will still be standing up. But to do this, you will need the strong belt of truth and the breastplate of God's approval. Wear shoes that are able to speed you on as you preach the Good News of peace with God. In every battle you will need faith as your shield to stop the fiery arrows aimed at you by Satan. And you will need the helmet of salvation and the sword of the Spirit-—which is the Word of God."*

After the message, I understood the meaning of the oppression I had experienced the preceding evening. It was a an illustration and confirmation of the morning's service. The Lord had allowed me to feel the SPIRITUAL WARFARE that is fought over the control of our minds. The tightening band was the location of my helmet of salvation.

# 54

# Open Their Eye:
## Chariots of Fire

Mil and I arrived at Evangelistic Temple several minutes early for the worship service. After we were seated in the sanctuary, my mind began to wander. I recalled many of the experiences that Mil and I had been led through under the leadership of a sovereign God.

Together, we have learned so much through these latter years. The knowledge that He knows my ever thought is the most sobering of all. I wonder what my life would be like if God had revealed Himself to me in such a powerful manner when I was sixteen years old or so.

One of my greatest desires is to encourage young people not to waste so much of their lives before they seek a completely committed life in Christ. These thoughts led me to pray, "Lord, I know you have revealed so much to Mil and me, for which we are truly thankful. Now, Lord, OPEN THE EYES OF THOSE ASSEMBLED HERE TONIGHT SO THAT WE MAY SEE YOU IN A VERY PERSONAL WAY!"

The church service began and the sermon text was read from 2 Kings 6:14-17:

"*So one night the king of Syria sent a great army with many chariots and horses to surround the city. When the prophet's servant got up early the next morning and went outside, there were troops, horses, and chariots everywhere.*

"*'Alas, my master, what shall we do now?' he cried out to Elisha. 'Don't be afraid!' Elisha told him. 'For our army is bigger than theirs!' Then Elisha prayed, 'LORD, OPEN HIS EYES AND LET HIM SEE!' and the Lord opened the young man's eyes so that he could see horses of fire and chariots of fire everywhere upon the mountain!*"

I am convinced the Lord inspired me to pray that prayer. It is His desire to reveal Himself to us, but we must ask. We have not seen Him in His power and glory because we haven't asked. We may not know how or when God will answer, but He will if you ask in faith.

Our nation is suffering now because of blind "Eyes." The first "I" is ignorance and the second "I" is indifference. You cannot have a personal relationship with someone you do not know.

A life without total commitment to Christ is wasted on the temporary and will produce only emptiness. But life can be very exciting if we allow God to guide us over, through, or around the mountains we may encounter.

# 55

# Al and Wilbert:
# GOD DIRECTS OUR PATHS

I met Wilbert at the Southern Hills Baptist Church in Tulsa. I knew him from the day he first stepped in the door. We had many conversations at church services, functions, and as passengers on the evening bus. Wilbert was an employee at one of the downtown banks.

Al was a civil engineer also employed in the downtown area. His ancestors were from India. He was another of the friends I made as I rode the Tulsa Transit System. All three of us lived very near one another in adjoining apartment complexes.

Al and Wilbert were about the same age, and neither was married. They were approximately thirty years younger than I. We often talked together as we walked from the bus stop to our homes. I guess that Wilbert's and my conversations regarding our mutual interests in our church happened so often that it gave Al the impression that we were excluding him.

One evening as Al I were riding home together, he said, "You and Wilbert aren't the only ones who believe in God. I believe in God too."

I replied, "I know that you do. In fact, many gods probably. The difference is the God I know is a personal God. He knows all about me, my needs, my thoughts—everything!

"When I have a problem, I can pray to him and He will hear me. He will give me direction as He wills. My God knows the future, so He already knows the answers to my questions before I even ask. He is concerned about anything that concerns me."

At about that time our bus arrived at the point where we exited the bus. Wilbert was also on the bus. I don't recall that I even knew he was before that moment. In any event, he had heard nothing of the conversation between Al and me. We exchanged greetings and started our walk. (This occurred during the time when many of the oil companies were leaving the Tulsa area. The economy was slumping rapidly, and as a result, many people were either being relocated or losing their jobs.)

Wilbert began our conversation. "Today, my office gave me a choice. The bank is going to downsize our staff. I have been given the option of resigning and receiving a big bonus or staying on, and if I have to be cut later, I will receive nothing extra."

Al, who had become a very close friend of Wilbert's, became very concerned. He asked, "What are you going to do? Doesn't that really upset you?"

Wilbert replied calmly, "No, no problem at all. I am going home and ask God which decision is best for me. He'll direct me to the right one."

I said nothing and listened as Wilbert shared his faith in God to Al. He reiterated much that I had said to Al earlier during our ride. God was confirming to me that He had heard every word that I had said to Al. It was a very pleasant time for me. Wilbert was the first to leave our group. As Al and I continued our way, I said, "Al, Wilbert did not hear our talk about a personal God, but he just confirmed that which I told you is true. This is not a coincidence. You have just witnessed the workings of a personal God who loves and is very concerned about you."

Al was very thoughtful for a time. Finally, he said, "I'm going to have to give this a lot of thought."

When I got home, I called Wilbert immediately and related to him the complete episode. I suggested to him, "Go get him. I think he is ready to listen. Take him someplace where he can be ministered to."

I know that Wilbert did take him to see a drama about creation, the Fall, and the purpose of Christ's death, burial, and resurrection. I never saw Al again after that. I have long wondered if he ever came to know God personally. I do know that God spoke to him through us.

# 56

# Flight:
## FAITHFULNESS

The pilot of our Oklahoma State University plane showed me the radar screen he was watching closely. There was a storm on each side of our route home to Stillwater. He assured those of us flying with him that he would land quickly if the corridor between the storms began to close.

Those in our party were members of a building committee that were preparing plans for a new physical education building on our campus. We had spent the previous night at the Columbus site of Ohio State University after we toured the structures that were of interest to our building program.

When we arose earlier that morning, it was pouring rain. Our pilot contacted the airport. Their weatherman said there had been some tornado damage in Illinois and that storm was moving in our direction. Behind the storm was a second front that could also pose some possible concern to us.

Our pilot was a veteran with many years of experience. He decided that after the first front passed us, we would take off and fly between the fronts or until it was no longer safe to proceed.

Now as we hurried home, I was seated next to a window. I was looking at the landscape below. It was indistinct in the gloomy atmosphere. We were flying just below some very heavy clouds. As I looked straight down, I saw a bolt of lightning that seemed to originate from under us and hit into the ground. All during this time, I was at peace, perfect peace.

The Presence of the Lord fell on me from almost the moment we had become airborne. I knew the Lord was telling me there was absolutely nothing to be concerned about. I knew He would be with us all of the way home as we flew between the two storm fronts. This sense of His Presence was very comforting.

When I got back home in Stillwater after the tiring trip, Mil was preparing our meal. I noticed *The Living Bible* on the table beside my chair. Almost unconsciously, I opened it up. The first verse I saw was Psalm 36:5. It read:

"Your steadfast love, O Lord, is as great as all the heavens. Your faithfulness reaches beyond the clouds."

Think about the psalmist who wrote this centuries ago. Do you not wonder what was on his mind as he wrote about faithfulness beyond the clouds. He could not have conceived at that time of my flying through a storm where I would be assured of the Lord's faithfulness. His Presence had filled the plane.

# 57

# Rose: $42

Rose, a widow lady, had a ministry of teaching young children. She worked in many communities around the state, giving parties for the youngsters and their mothers. She had developed many props to keep their attention as she taught the Word of God. She was supported by many churches of different denominations. Each church supplied a different one of her needs such as rent, utilities, groceries, car, and gas.

The Sunday school class of which Mil was a member took up an offering each week for Rose's spending money. Mil was responsible for collecting spending money and informing her class of Rose's ministry. The ladies usually gave between twelve and twenty dollars each week. Mil and I took the contribution to Rose on the following Monday or Tuesday.

One particular Sunday morning, the offering was forty-two dollars and some odd cents. When the morning service was over, Mil told me about the larger than normal offering. She insisted that Rose must have some have unknown financial emergency.

She believed we should take the money to Rose without delay. When we arrived at Roses's home, she wasn't there, so Mil put the cash in an envelope and slipped it in her mail box.

Shortly afterward, Mil received a note from Rose to be read to her Sunday school class. It read that while on one of her trips out of town, her car had broken down. A mechanic in the city of her mishap had given her his labor free when he heard of her plight. However, there was a bill for his parts in the amount of forty-two dollars.

Rose assured the mechanic that she would mail him that amount—God would provide the funds. The first thing she saw as she entered her home when she returned was the envelope. In it was the dollar amount needed to pay for the parts required to repair her car, plus the change needed for the stamp to mail the payment. She wanted the members of the class to know how God had blessed her and would bless them for their sensitivity to hear God speak to them of her need.

# 58

# Salt:
## Witness

In the first months of 1997, I had another dream. Unlike dreams of the past that usually have dealt with a new truth or a direction for my life, this one dealt with a warning for the Christians of this nation if we are to overcome the corruption that has impregnated our culture like a cancer.

I dreamed I was carrying multicolored grains of white, blue, and green sand in a large bowl. I poured it into low places in the ground. As I was pouring, I saw some white powder spill out of this material. I knew that it was cyanide poison.

I was alarmed that a child or an animal might come into contact with the poison and possibly be harmed. I wondered what I could do to remedy the situation. It was then that I saw a row of crockery pots about ten inches high and five inches in diameter.

The pots were spaced about three feet apart. I looked inside of a pot and saw that it was filled with salt. I decided that the salt would neutralize the poison. As I made this decision, the dream ended. I awoke and began to think about the meaning of the dream, but nothing came to my mind.

It was Sunday morning, and I remembered that John Hagee, pastor of the Cornerstone Church of San Antonio, Texas would be on television at that time. When I tuned in to his service, he was talking about, "The Salt Covenant."

I knew immediately that the dream was from the Lord, but nothing in the dream seemed to connect with his sermon. I studied the salt covenant, but I found nothing that helped me understand what God was saying.

As I analyzed the dream, I began to wonder if the cyanide represented the sin in this world, the multicolored sand represented the various races of the world, and the salt was the solution for the dilemmas of these times. This reasoning made some sense, but there was no confirmation of these thoughts.

I could not get rid of a feeling of urgency that it was very important, not only for me, but the people of this land.

A short time later, I noticed a special book among our own personal collection. It was *Vine's Expository Dictionary of New Testament Words*. I looked up "salt". The following are excerpts from the definition:

SALT-
*Being possessed of purifying, perpetuating, and antiseptic qualities.*
*Emblematic of fidelity and friendship among eastern nations.*
*Emblematic of the covenant between God and His people. Numbers, 18:19 [John Hagee's sermon topic]*
*In the Lord's teaching, it is symbolic of that spiritual health and vigor essential to Christian virtue and counteractive to the corruption that is in this world.*

I knew I had found the confirmation I had been searching for. I knew my theory as to the meaning of the dream was correct. I went on to read two reference scriptures:

"You are the salt of the earth, but if the salt loses its saltiness, how can it be made salty again? It is no longer good for anything except to be thrown out and trampled by men" (Matthew 5:13).

"Let your conversation be always full of grace, seasoned with salt, so that you may know how to answer everyone" (Colossians 4:6).

It is now very clear what the Lord was saying. The only answer for the problems of this country is for those who are called by His name to become salt, so I began to record my thoughts on paper. I arose during the middle of a Saturday night and began to write about Uncle Clarence, Aunt Flora, and Grandma Shumate.

They surely personified salty people as described in those two verses. They were faithful and completely committed to the Lord. They were never overbearing in their witness, and their conversation was always full of grace and seasoned with salt. And maybe most of all, they were a joy to be around at all times. Aunt Flora's life was proof that God was the author of good humor.

The next morning, I tuned in to Adrian Rogers, a Baptist minister at the First Baptist Church in Nashville, Tenn. When he announced that his sermon was to be about "salt," I knew that God was going to speak to me through this man. His sermon was based on the same verses as the ones I had read the previous night.

He stressed the need for Christians to become the salt of the earth. He stated that neither the government nor any other institution had a solution for our country's woes. Christ is the only answer we have.

The sermon was a solid confirmation to me that my dream was serving as God's warning to this society if we are to survive our present alarming social conditions. I do not believe that the Lord would have given this picture to me if He was not providing an answer for our survival. It is obvious that the row of salt-filled pots is not being put to use.

My prayer for each of you is that you will acquire a pot of salt and that you will learn to use it at every opportunity to glorify God.

# 59

# Dream:
## NAKED AND UNASHAMED

I had another dream a few days following the dream concerning the salt. This dream lasted only for a period of a few seconds. It was a picture that I found disgusting to my senses. There was no movement and no word of knowledge.

I did not think that it could be from the Lord. I tried to reject it from my mind because it related to a person I knew personally. For this reason, I am reticent to say very much about the dream lest someone misinterpret the symbolism.

Two or three days later, I still could not understand the message of the picture. That evening as I was viewing a Christian television station, a visiting pastor was introduced. The host asked him about his present work.

At almost that exact instant, the troubling dream came to my mind. The pastor, T.D. Jakes, said that he had finished a new book. He called it *NAKED and Not Ashamed*. That was a perfect description of the title that I would have given the apparition that was causing me so much unrest.

I understood for the first time the message of the dream. The person was naked and unashamed. She represents in her adultery the wickedness and idolatry in our present day society. It is growing with each successive generation. The person personified in the dream was Gomer, the unfaithful wife of Hosea. She was a living illustration to Israel of that nation's unfaithfulness in playing a harlot with other gods. Our country was, as was Israel in its founding, dedicated to God. However, with each blessing He has given us, we have moved further away from Him. We have separated our government and our schools, our very lives from His sovereign guidance.

Determine the idols that have become a part of your life. Make a list of every component of your life in the order of its importance to you. Insert the point at which your committed relationship to God occurs. Every item that is more important to you is an idol. It is an idol of more importance to you than your respect and love for God.

God says in Romans 1:21, *"Yes, they knew about him all right, but they wouldn't admit it or worship him or even thank him for all his daily care. And after awhile they began to think up silly ideas of what God was like and what he wanted them to do. The result was that their foolish minds became dark and confused.*

*Claiming themselves to be wise without God, they became utter fools instead. And then, instead of worshiping the glorious ever-living God, they took wood and stone and made idols for themselves, carving them to look like mere birds and animals and snakes and puny men."*

The results of this idolatry was written in Romans 1:24.25: *"So God let them go ahead into every sort of sex sin, and do whatever they wanted to-yes, vile and sinful things with each other's bodies. Instead of believing what they knew was the truth about God, they deliberately chose to believe lies. So they prayed to the things God made, but wouldn't obey the blessed God who made these things."*

Our country stands naked and unashamed. Without shame, our country will not repent. Without repentance, our country has no future. Without a future, our country has no hope. We find hope only in a person that we can trust. Trust in our leadership is paramount if we are to continue to be a blessed nation. Our only true trust and hope lies in the one who created us for His glory.

It is only as I conclude writing this book that I understand the purpose for the dreams, visions and other experiences dating back to 1975 of which I am a witness. I found the answer as I read Hosea 12:10, 11.

*"I sent my prophets to warn you with many a vision and many a parable and dream. But the sins of Gilgal flourish just the same. Row on row of altars-like furrows in afield-are used for sac-*

*rifices to your idols. And Gilead, too, is full of fools who worship idols."*

Gilgal was the center of idol worship in Israel. Our country is full of fools who worship idols. As he warned Israel, He is warning us in like manner of our idolatry and the consequences that will result if we do not repent.

# 60

## THE TABLE IS SET

I remember nothing about the church service at Evangelistic Temple that morning, except for a vision that lasted for perhaps two seconds. I saw the end of a dining table located about twenty-five feet from me. The other end was invisible because the table was so long that the other end disappeared into the horizon. The table was prepared for a banquet. All the dishes and serving bowls were set in place. The only thing lacking were the guests who had been invited to the feast. To explain this vision is not difficult. It is described in Revelation 19:6, 7.

"Then I heard again what sounded like the shouting of a huge crowd, or like the waves of a hundred oceans crashing on the shore, or like the mighty rolling of greater thunder, 'Praise the Lord. For the Lord our God, the Almighty, reigns. Let us be glad and rejoice and honor him; for the time has come for the wedding banquet of the Lamb, and his bride has prepared herself. She is permitted to wear the cleanest and whitest and finest of linens.' (Fine linen represents the good deeds done by the people of God.)

"And the angel dictated this sentence to me: 'Blessed are those who are invited to the Wedding Feast of the Lamb.' And he added, 'God himself has stated this.'"

To the reader of this story, I strongly suggest that if you haven't received your invitation as yet, then make a reservation immediately. The menu will be out of this world. The guest of honor, Jesus, is beyond description. The celebration will last forever. If you know anyone that you desire to bring with you, the guest list is open for a little longer, and you can guarantee your friends that they will in no way be disappointed.

# Epilogue

I wish I had kept a diary since 1975. It never occurred to me in years past that I would ever write the preceding stories. I have done so now only because of the encouragement of three people.

They all asked me the same question, "Are you writing your stories down?"

They each gave a different reason for my doing so. Uncle Clarence Plannett was the first to suggest that I should be recording the stories as a history for my family if for no other purpose. A young lady, employed at the Lakeside Golf Club, whose name I don't recall, was the second. She found the stories to be a source of knowledge.

When the third person, James Beauchamp, an attorney in Tulsa, asked me the same question and answered it himself with, "I think you should be recording them. I find them very encouraging,"" I decided to at least make an attempt.

As I began to write, the Lord began to track my stories with many signs and wonders too numerous to mention. One evening I finished the outline of all of stories I had indexed to write. I noticed that it was time for me to take my nightly medication, so I went to get my pill in another room and closed the door behind me. As I was taking it, I heard a voice in the area that I had just left. It was an audible voice, a voice that seemed to originate from about three feet in front of me.

I heard a very firm masculine voice say, "WILLIAM, I READ YOUR BOOK." I wondered who had come into the other room so late in the evening and could have read a book that I had finished outlining only a few a moments before. When I opened the door, there was no one there. He had called me "William."

No one calls me that, even though that it is my given name. My friends call me "Bill." In my spirit, I knew I had heard the audible voice of the Lord. I wondered why He had not said whether it was a good or a bad book. This question continued to concern me for a number of months, for I have never felt that I could adequately express with my limited vocabulary the incidents that I have witnessed.

I deliberated whether or not to continue. Now I know why He did not answer my inquiry. God does not inspire anything that is bad, nor is He impressed with the events that originate with Him. The only thing I can do to impress the Lord is to be obedient to Him and wholly follow Him in every circumstance.

In retrospect, the first and final events recorded are the most important. The first establishes the time period in which we are living. Although no ones knows the time when Jesus will return, the signs of His return are clear.

This is the time of the latter rain. Dreams, visions, and prophesying are occurring in ever increasing numbers. Israel, God's time clock, has become a nation again. Many of its citizens have returned on the wings of "eagles" as foretold centuries ago. The temple grounds are no longer occupied with Gentiles—we are a part of the last generation, and I strongly believe that some of us will witness the return of Jesus.

The last stories are a description of our country in its present state. It is a country that has lost its direction on the day that we separated our church of Jesus Christ from our government. We no longer have any absolute standard for our lives. Where there is no standard there can be nothing but confusion. We can easily be deceived when we have an ever changing system based on humanistic values.

But we are not without hope. The Lord says that greater is He [the Holy Spirit] that is within us than he that is within the world. The dream about the salt indicates that the body of Christ must become salt to overcome the poison or sin that is permeating this world. Salt neutralizes poison.

The stories in between the first and last are examples of the limitless ways that God can overcome any problem we might have. I have witnessed many more events, dreams, and visions than I have not recorded. I believe that I have submitted evidence that the Bible *IS* The Inspired Word Of God and is true and in perfect time in every detail. Continuing to write more happenings would not add any further substantiation of His power to speak to those who have an ear to hear what the Spirit is saying.

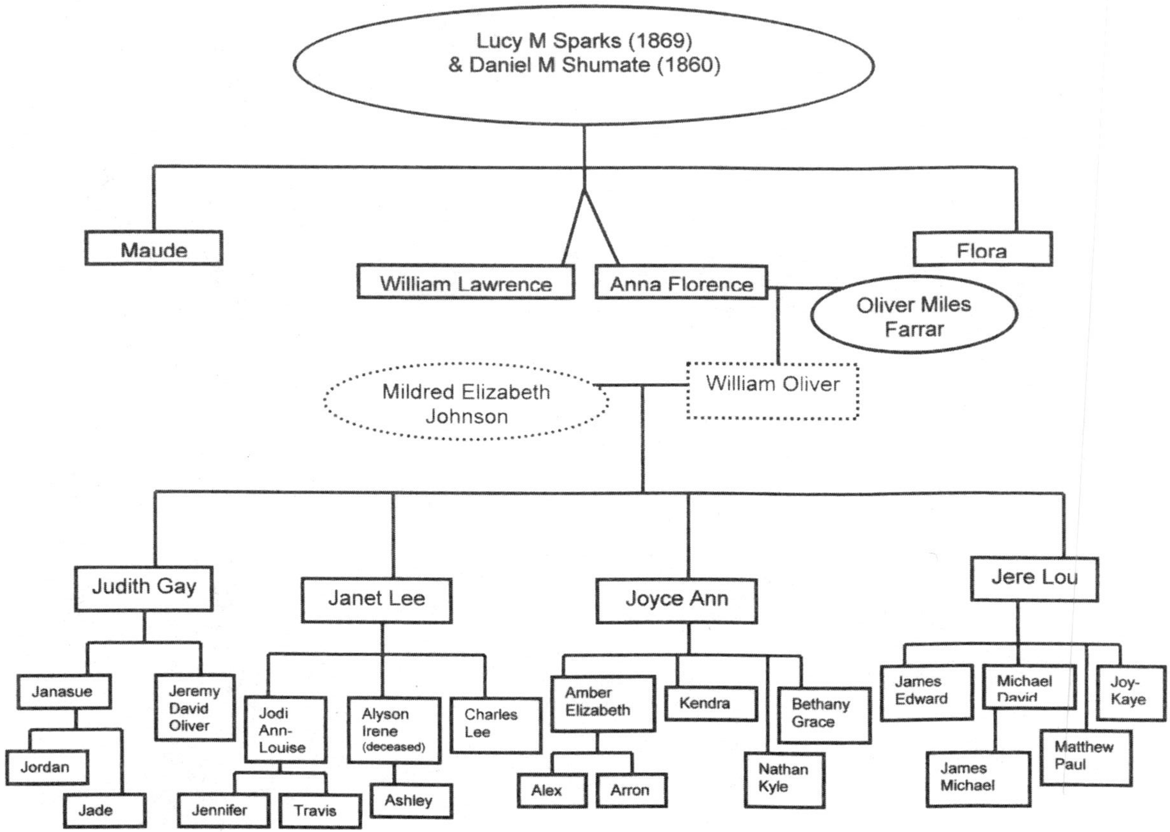
Lucy M Sparks (1869)
& Daniel M Shumate (1860)
Maude
William Lawrence
Anna Florence
Flora
Oliver Miles Farrar
William Oliver
Mildred Elizabeth Johnson
Judith Gay
Janet Lee
Joyce Ann
Jere Lou
Janasue
Jeremy David Oliver
Jordan
Jade
Jodi Ann-Louise
Alyson Irene (deceased)
Charles Lee
Jennifer
Travis
Ashley
Amber Elizabeth
Kendra
Bethany Grace
Nathan Kyle
Alex
Arron
James Edward
Michael David
Joy-Kaye
Matthew Paul
James Michael

# Order Form

**Postal orders:**
Bill Farrar, 2820 South Washington, Stillwater, OK 74074
    e-mail: aprilrain@mail.provalue.net

**Telephone orders:** (405) 624-1831

**Please send** *William I Read Your Book* **to:**

Name:_____

Address:_____

City:_____ State:_____

Zip:_____

Telephone: (____) _____


**Book Price:** $14.99 in U.S. dollars.

**Sales Tax:** Please add 8.25% for books shipped to a Oklahoma address.

**Shipping:** $3.00 for the first book and $2.00 for each additional book to cover shipping and handling within US, Canada, and Mexico. International orders add $7.00 for the first book and $3.00 for each additional book.


Quantity Discounts Available - Please call for information
(405) 624-1831